Anonymous

Half Hour in the Far North

Life amid snow and ice

Anonymous

Half Hour in the Far North
Life amid snow and ice

ISBN/EAN: 9783337254186

Printed in Europe, USA, Canada, Australia, Japan

Cover: Foto ©ninafisch / pixelio.de

More available books at **www.hansebooks.com**

HALF HOURS
IN THE FAR NORTH

"EREBUS" AND "TERROR."

See Page 243.

THE HALF HOUR LIBRARY
OF TRAVEL, NATURE AND SCIENCE
FOR YOUNG READERS.

HALF HOURS N THE FAR NORTH

Life amid Snow and Ice

WITH NUMEROUS ILLUSTRATIONS

LONDON
DALDY, ISBISTER, & CO.
56, LUDGATE HILL
1878

LONDON:
PRINTED BY VIRTUE AND CO., LIMITED,
CITY ROAD.

CONTENTS.

ICELAND.

CHAP.		PAGE
I.	THE ISLAND	3
II.	THE DESERT	23
III.	THE PEOPLE	39

NORTHERN RUSSIA.

I.	THROUGH THE BALTIC	55
II.	CRONSTADT	66
III.	ST. PETERSBURG	75
IV.	MOSCOW	99
V.	MANNERS AND CUSTOMS	115

GREENLAND.

I.	THE COAST	131
II.	FREDERIKSHAAB	138
III.	HOLSTEINBORG	151
IV.	GODHAVEN	160

ORKNEY.

CHAP.		PAGE
I.	SCENERY OF THE GROUP	171
II.	OCCUPATION OF THE PEOPLE	184

SHETLAND.

I.	LERWICK	197
II.	FAIR ISLE AND FOULA	206

ARCTIC SEAS.

I.	SEARCH FOR FRANKLIN	219
II.	SEARCH FOR FRANKLIN	232
III.	SEARCH FOR FRANKLIN	248

NORWAY.

I.	THE LAND	263
II.	THE NATIVES AT HOME	278
III.	THE NATIVES ABROAD	290
IV.	DAY AND NIGHT	296

LIST OF ILLUSTRATIONS.

	PAGE
"EREBUS" AND "TERROR" .	*Frontispiece.*
REYKJAVIK, THE CAPITAL OF ICELAND	7
MOUNT HECKLA	11
THE GREAT GEYSER	17
THE STROKR	21
THE RIVER JOKULSA . .	25
THE GREAT NORTHERN DIVER	29
LANDSCAPE IN THE DESERT	33
AN "INN" ON THE TRACK	36
TRAVELLING IN ICELAND	41
INTERIOR OF A HOUSE	44
BIRD-CATCHING	49
FISHING-SMACK	57
ELSINEUR	59
THE DROSKY	69
RUSSIAN VOSTICK, BEGGAR, AND PRIEST . .	73
ON THE NEVA IN WINTER	79

LIST OF ILLUSTRATIONS.

	PAGE
THE MAMMOTH	82
THE CZAR AND KARL	91
MAP OF ST. PETERSBURG AND THE ISLANDS	96
PEASANTS' HOUSES	97
RUSSIAN TEA-SELLERS	100
THE CATHEDRAL OF ST. BASIL	103
THE GREAT BELL OF MOSCOW	105
MOSCOW	107
A RUSSIAN SUMMER CARRIAGE	119
WORKMEN AT DINNER	125
THE SPITZBERGEN ICE-STREAM	136
INHABITANTS OF GREENLAND	139
ESKIMO HUTS	143
THE INTERIOR IN SUMMER	146
SEAL-HUNTING ON ICE-FIELDS	149
DANISH SETTLEMENT AT HOLSTEINBORG	153
THE HALO	156
THE DOG-SLEDGE	159
THE AURORA BOREALIS	163
HUNTING THE SEAL	165
THE WALRUS	167
THE STENNIS STONES	175
A PICTS' HOUSE	177
EGG-GATHERING	187
AN ORKNEY FARMHOUSE	191
GIRL AND BOY OF THE BETTER CLASS	200
THE FISHERMAN'S GALLOP	203
THE COAST	207
THE CRADLE OF NOSS	210
HOMES OF THE POORER CLASS	213
SHETLAND FISHING-BOAT	215
WHALERS IN BAFFIN'S BAY	222
WINTER IN WELLINGTON CHANNEL	225
DRAGGING BOAT ACROSS ICE-FIELDS	228

LIST OF ILLUSTRATIONS.

	PAGE
POLAR BEARS	235
THE EDGE OF A PACK	238
SUMMER IN LANCASTER SOUND	241
AN ESKIMO VILLAGE	245
DISCOVERY AT THE ROSS CAIRN	251
ARCTIC BIRDS	257
AMONG THE ISLANDS	266
ENTRANCE TO A FIORD	269
A FIORD SEEN FROM ABOVE	272
A COAST GLACIER	275
A NORWEGIAN CARRIAGE	279
PEASANTS AND MINISTER	282
AT THE HEAD OF THE NORD FIORD	285
NORWEGIAN DANCE	288
AN HOUR AFTER MIDNIGHT	299
THE EAGLE	305
MOUNTAIN SCENERY	308

ICELAND.

ICELAND.

CHAPTER I.

THE ISLAND.

I HAVE certainly, in all my wanderings, never sailed over a more desolate and stormy sea than that which lies between Great Britain and Iceland. In the voyages both out and home we were constantly beset by violent gales. Only once were we cheered by the sight of a ship, and she was scudding with close-reefed sails before a pitiless storm. Day after day there was the same sweltering of the waters, the same threatening sky and warning barometer.

The evening we left Liverpool everything promised well. The sun set in great beauty over the Isle of Man. The distant horizon was dimly hedged in by the purple coast of Ireland, and on the calm sea a large fleet of herring-boats with drooping sails shot their nets in the glowing light. Removed from all comparison with the leviathans of the Mersey, our little steamer grew upon us till we had almost forgotten the hesitation we at first felt to encounter the North Atlantic in such a tiny craft.

As night closed, a stormy petrel hovered about us; but all on sky and sea appeared so calm and peaceable, and the big solemn barometer seemed so confident of fine weather, that we derided our little enemy as a hopeless lunatic who should be bound over to keep the peace towards us. However, Mother Carey's envoy, as usual, knew more than we did of what the winds and waves were meditating, and though at night the barometer hastened to rectify his prognostic, and courageously threw a somersault from fair to foul, he was hardly in time to "assist" at the commencement of the strife.

In the morning after leaving port, we passed the south end of Islay, and saw its beetling crags lashed by spindrift as the grey swirls of rain-cloud were rent for a moment by the rising gale. That was our last sight of land till we made Iceland after five days severe buffeting with the wind and sea. For a day or two the gale came roaring up after us

"With all
Its stormy crests that smoked against the sky,"

and bore us bravely on into the dark waste of waters, walled by mist, which lay beyond; and I confess this part of our voyage was very enjoyable. It was most pleasing to watch the graceful gliding of the great waves, which one moment ready to topple on the head of the seaman lashed to the wheel, noiselessly slid below us to dash out beneath the bows in a broad glittering carpet of foam.

When we had been carried hopelessly beyond any harbour of refuge, far out near Rockhall, the following gale ceased, and after a short interval of tumbled repose we encountered a "whole gale" right in our teeth, which compelled us to "lie to" for many hours in a sea as wildly tumultuous as it has ever been my lot to encounter.

The little ship fought bravely. At one moment, reared on her hind legs, she menaced the coming seas; at the next, almost standing on her head, she dived into the deep trough which divided them, and again rolling from side to side, nearly sent her funnel and masts overboard. She certainly met most of the rollers fiercely, but occasionally a great seahorse with a crest of foam would rise and strike her such a blow that every fibre of her frame trembled. It was as if old Tor was trying to beat us back from his ancient realm with heavy strokes of his mighty hammer.

How the heart leaps when that terrible crash comes overhead caused by a heavy sea on deck! For a time the ship appears completely crushed by the blow, and unable again to rise from the trough into which she sinks. But up she comes again, as buoyant as a cork, and you breathe more freely till you instinctively know that it is time for another alarm. The regular rhythm of the waves is very remarkable. For hours I could tell within a second or two in what direction the ship would next pitch, and how the approaching wave would strike her.

At last, on the afternoon of the fifth day, the sailors discovered land in what seemed to us landsmen a thick storm cloud.

A high bank of darkness to the north blended sea and sky, but gradually out of this blackness indistinct forms of rocks became perceptible. At first they appeared no more than denser portions of the darkness, but at last, from the shroud-like covering, tremendous precipices, rising at a bound from the foaming breakers beneath, could be clearly made out, their summits crowned by snow and their high valleys filled with glancing ice-streams. As the flying clouds were borne rapidly across their precipitous faces, and the ocean swell broke hoarsely on their base, a more inhospitable or dangerous looking coast could not well be imagined.

We sailed between the Westmann Islands and the southern coast of Iceland. The islands referred to are volcanic masses thrown out into the sea, and linked together by low reefs over which the foaming breakers were driving madly.

Here we first encountered the whale, which is so common an inhabitant of these seas. On our way home thirty of them were at one time visible from the deck. In mist and rain, with a strong southerly breeze and

rising sea, we ran along a lee shore, low, dark, and precipitous, where no place of refuge could be found for a luckless ship unable to hold her own. Our sixty horses worked away bravely, but if they had become restive there is little doubt what the result would have been.

Occasionally we caught a glimpse of the jagged and pinnacled hills of the interior, their size and gloomy character enhanced by their covering of clouds; but generally a low-lying, black, lifeless shore, guarded by projecting reefs and fiercely beaten by surf, was what we alone saw during this our first introduction to Iceland. We had to steer a good deal by the fitful light of the breakers, out and in, keeping them in sight.

We passed the "Smoky Cape" after sunset, and well it deserves its name. Against its iron face, round its basaltic columns, and deep into its wild caverns, the waves, urged on by the southern gale, broke themselves into fragments of foam, and shot up in long tongues of brilliant white. There could not have been a more imposing or appropriate welcome to a land we had all pictured as the abode of storm, ice, and fire. I involuntarily repeated the well-known lines—

"A waste land where no one comes,
Or hath come since the making of the world."

If I had seen nothing more of Iceland than that gloomy picture, I should have carried away a very different impression of it from what I received a few days afterwards, when I rode along the same coast and saw it steeped in the brightest sunshine, and when these same weird-like hills stood out clear and purple against a sky as transparent as any Italian one.

Nowhere is the traveller more dependent on weather than in Iceland. Having to live in wooden churches or tents without fire, the existence of sunshine or rain makes all possible difference to his comfort. The climate generally deals in extremes, and if not overwhelmed with ruthless rain, you are baked in sunshine.

We had one day's experience of the true orthodox rain of the country, and I should never care again to be exposed to it. Cold sleety rain and wind, which pierced even to one's very marrow, was not the best discipline for a preserved meat dinner innocent of fire, and a bivouac under dripping canvass. But when the sun poured forth in splendour over the splintered rocks and wonderfully coloured hills, lighting up the icy summits of the Jokülls with a golden haze, and pencilling the clouds with the most delicate tints of beauty, and filling the green valleys with light and colour, and the air with that elasticity and joy known to every traveller in Switzerland, then the rain and the wind were forgotten in the all-pervading pleasure of existence.

It is to its volcanos that Iceland owes its chief and most characteristic feature. In no part of the world is such dire destruction or such terrible evidence of this fearful agency seen.

THE ISLAND.   11

Most of the greater mountains have been, or are still, volcanos; and in truth the whole island owes its birth to volcanic upheaval. So rough, so wild and rugged, is the land, that it appears like a fragment torn from the bottom

MOUNT HECKLA.

of the deep, and elevated above the waves by some convulsion of nature.

Heckla is the volcano best known, because it lies to the south of the island, and can be seen by passing ships, but it is very far from being the most destructive of the "Eruptors" of Iceland. On an average, there has been an explosion somewhere in the island every thirteen years, and several of these have been unsurpassed for their violent and devastating effects.

It is very remarkable that in a land where bravery and enterprise have never been wanting, a region some 3,000 square miles in extent, lying in the south-east corner of the island, should never have been penetrated by man. In that wild and untrodden desert stand some of the most destructive craters.

Age after age, wave upon wave of burning lava has been poured over it, earthquakes have rent it and tormented it, without the eye of man ever resting on its mysteries. From out of this solitude, perfect seas of molten lava have, at various times, flowed over the pastures and laboriously cultivated fields of the wretched inhabitants. Considerable hills have been thrown up, water-courses cut deep in the hills filled full to the brim, and long reefs and islands cast far out into the sea.

One stream is 50 miles long, 15 miles broad, and 600 feet deep; and it has been calculated that one volcano in that wilderness threw out, during one eruption, fifty to sixty millions of cubic yards of material! Into the inhabited regions alone a greater bulk than Mont Blanc was projected!

The accounts which have been handed down of this event present to us a picture too terrible almost for belief. With a widespread destruction of the land, the depths of the sea were invaded, and the fish (the Icelanders' chief means of subsistence) driven from the shore. The flames broke out even through the waves in the line of movement, and the sea was covered with pumice for 150 miles.

A thick canopy hung over the island for a year, and the winds carried the ashes over Europe, Africa, and America. The very sun was darkened, and showed only as a ball of fire, while frightful hurricanes, hail-storms, thunder and lightning added their horrors, and famine and pestilence still further reduced the number of those who survived the catastrophe.

The great lava streams are inconceivably wild. A sight of one is a sufficient reward for crossing the ocean. A more complete "abomination of desolation" cannot else be found.

To describe such a stream as like a billowy sea arrested in its wildest frenzy and turned into stone, would give but a faint notion of the fretted turbulent twistings, deep rents and chasms, threatening pinnacles, and overhanging crests of dull cindery lava, which, ghost-like, stretch to the horizon.

Sometimes extraordinary swirls in the rock show how the viscous mass was moved while it cooled. Large corrugated surfaces thus frequently occur, and occasionally they even assume patterns like a tesselated pavement.

Sometimes you pass over broad domes that ring to the

tread, and beneath subterranean chambers stretch to a great distance, which might serve as dens for all the wild beasts of the forest. Hidden from the summer sun, banks of ice and snow lie in some of these caves all the year round; and small holes, into which a horse's foot is apt to slide, are a constant source of danger to the traveller.

The persistent heat of these masses of lava is evidenced by the fact, that many years after their effusion they continue hot and smoking.

Such sterile, howling wildernesses are what Rachel would have fitly termed "a sublime horror." Hardly a trace of life in animal or plant is met with.

The lowest lichens and a weather-beaten grey moss sear the rocks with faint traces of colour, and at long intervals an eagle, or one of the apoplectic ravens which haunt these solitudes, may flit noiselessly past, their dark shadow gliding like an evil spirit over the barren rocks. Not another sign of life exists, and, in truth, the absence of insect life is one of the most curious and striking features of the country. Except in some of the valleys by the side of rivers, where hungry gnats abound, there is hardly a winged insect to be seen.

No bees or butterflies fill the air with their busy hum, or pass glittering down the breeze. There are no hedgerows or copses "melodious with tune," no little birds impetuous with song. On the moors the melancholy cry of the plover may at intervals be heard, but the thrush and starling and corncrake never come in all that silent land.

Among the grass and stones few worms or little insects meet your eye. I saw no beetle, or spider, or snail. The very house-fly did not visit our tent; and certain heavy and light cavalry, so common in the houses of more southern lands, are, so far as I could learn, prudently indifferent to so cold and unpromising a field of industry and enterprise as is presented to them in Iceland.

Everywhere a strange silence reigns, like that of the Great Desert. Over head and under foot everything wears the lifeless silence of desolation. It is in winter that the echoes are aroused, and then, with the hurricane "travelling in the greatness of his strength," and the ice artillery, the long valleys and iron hills shout again.

Craters of all sizes are very commonly met with. Occasionally, a few yards from the road, you can look down a black funnel into an unknown abyss; sometimes an unfathomable lake occupies an old vent; and I have heard of filled-up craters serving as sheep-folds. But it is not lava alone which is projected from the subterranean chambers of Iceland. Hot mud, boiling water, liquid sulphur, are at different places thrown up; and it is especially in those valleys, where the discoloured sloughs of sulphur smudge the ground and streak the hillside, and where the vapours of boiling cauldrons constantly fill the air, that you fully realise your near approach to the "ignes suppositi," and feel disposed to examine suspiciously all the hollows and lurking places for the befitting genius.

The hot springs of Iceland have been for ages celebrated, and some of them have even ranked among the seven wonders of the world. I was so fortunate as to witness a very successful performance of the Great Geyser (*i.e.* Gusher), and congratulate myself on the same, as in his old age he is becoming less fond of display, and has even remained gloomy and taciturn while Prince Napoleon and his photographers and painters and mathematicians were standing ready for days to picture, measure, and immortalise him.

Geysers are very common in Iceland. They may be frequently seen steaming away like energetic pots in the plains, and waving their white flags in the breeze. Sometimes they obligingly throw their hot water into the icy lakes, and doubtless thereby gladden the cold toes of the fish; sometimes they bubble and boil deep down below ground, in dark holes of unpleasant aspect.

In the valley of "Hawk-dale," where *the* Geyser presides, it is said above one hundred hot springs are found; but only a few of them are in any way remarkable. Most of these are placed on the slope of a low hill of slaty tuffa, which rises to a height of about three hundred feet above the valley; and from the summit of this hill a most beautiful view is got, not only of the boiling springs below, but also of the long green valley, with its many rivers and purple ridges of bordering hills, immediately beyond which towers the double cone of Heckla, and the range of dome-shaped Jokülls on either side.

Near the base of this hill there is a most beautiful,

THE GREAT GEYSER.

delicately tinted cavern, with bossy **walls, full to the brim
with boiling** water, **which is as** clear **as crystal, and
entirely devoid of** taste or smell. This **is the favourite
cooking-pot of** travellers. It makes admirable tea ; **and
we anchored in** its depths sundry tin cans and sausages,
whose flavour afterwards seemed exquisite to our hungry
palates.

This fountain was at one time the chief eruptor, but
after an earthquake it ceased **to play,** and made over
the performance **to the Great Geyser,** which then began.

The " **Great Geyser** " **has built up for itself a truncated**
conical mound, **by the deposit of** the silicious **material so
largely** held in suspension **by its waters.**

On the summit of this mound **stands the saucer-shaped
basin, in the centre of** which **the crater or** pipe **opens.**
The **basin is** about **four** feet deep at the **edge of** the
crater, but shallows gradually to the lip. It measures
above seventy feet across, and the pipe is about ten feet in
diameter, and perfectly smooth within, where it has been
polished by the constant rush of the boiling water. The
basin is always full, **except** for a short **interval after an
eruption,** when it is **emptied, and then you** can walk **into**
the edge of the crater, **over** the **hot** stone, and look **down**
the pipe **at the** fiercely boiling flood, filling gradually **up**
again to its old **level.**

When **full the basin looks very** beautiful, from the
clearness **of the** water and the deep blue colour of the
pipe. **The water is always** boiling, and large bubbles of
air rise **to the** surface **from the unknown regions below.**

The interior of the basin is rough, like cerebral coral or cauliflower, and plants thrown into the water become covered by silicious encrustation.

We witnessed a grand display, after many false alarms, during which an abortive attempt was apparently made by the master of the ceremonies to gratify us. With a slight tremor of the earth, and considerable groaning and sighing, a water-column, or rather, I should say, a sheaf of columns, rose higher and higher out of the basin. These columns partially sank again and again, but continued at each renewed effort to gain greater altitude, till, with a final attempt, a maximum of about one hundred feet was reached. This height was only maintained for a few seconds, and down like a telescope the whole mass sank, the entire period consumed in the display being seven minutes and a half.

The explosion was accompanied by so much steam, that the water-column was greatly concealed; still it was a very wonderful and gratifying spectacle. As throb after throb raised the dome of water higher and higher, the excitement among the spectators was, as may be believed, very great.

At one time the Geyser is said to have been much more powerful than in our day, and to have risen between three and four hundred feet every six hours; but that was in his hot and fiery youth: he is now old and feeble, and gradually builds up a flinty tomb, which one day will enclose him as similar formations have done not a few of his brethren.

The Lesser Geyser erupts at short intervals, but to no great height; while the "Strokr" (*i.e.* "Churn"), the remaining hot spring of chief interest in this locality, is of such an excitable disposition that he can be roused to activity by a trick, and made to contribute to the amusement of every passer.

THE STROKR.

At a depth of twelve feet from the surface, this Geyser, when quiescent, pursues his boiling trade with not a little sound and fury; but as his throat is very narrow, it can easily be closed, and so our friend choked. This ignoble act is achieved by throwing in a few shovelfuls of sod. Naturally enough, he warmly resents such liberties being taken with his windpipe, and thus no sooner has the guide hurled in the proper dose, than, like a man with quinsy, the Strokr hisses and splutters, gasps and grumbles, till he can no longer contain himself, and up it all comes, boiling water, steam, and earth, in explosion after explosion, till the whole "ingesta" have been got quit of, and his pipe is again clear.

After many efforts and much excitement, he appears for a moment to calm, but again, apparently after thinking over it, he cannot brook the recollection, and at it he goes, almost as energetically as ever. He is a great performer is this Strokr; he would, I am sure, make the fortune of any showman who could tame and carry him to the Palace at Sydenham. On the whole, I think that if the water were clear, the eruption of the Strokr is more graceful, as it is nearly as high, as that of the Great Geyser.

ICELAND.

CHAPTER II.

THE DESERT.

THE central deserts of Iceland are unexplored. A man must be bold, and singularly favoured by weather, to investigate their mysterious recesses and to return with life.

One region, part wild tumbled snow and glacier mountains, part plains of bristling lava, is as unknown as the heart of Africa. The glimmer of silver peaks has been seen from afar across an impassable arm of lava, the confines of the great sea of molten matter have been skirted, but those billows of black ragged stone have never been traversed even in the old adventuresome days of Iceland.

Sometimes violent shocks and a rising column of black cloud warn distant settlers that volcanic fires are still active in the heart of that fearful wilderness; then the one great river Jökulsá, which flows from its mysterious depths, is tinged with volcanic ash, and swollen with melted snows; then, too, the night sky gleams scarlet over some unvisited, unknown, yawning crater, which is pouring forth its flood of molten rock.

This sea of lava sweeps up to the roots of a chain of snow mountains perfectly unexplored, themselves volcanos ready to toss aside their mantles of white and spread destruction for miles round.

To the west of this vast region of lava and snow lies an upland desert of black sparkling sand, stretching completely across the island. This sand is volcanic, and has been deposited during outbursts of the neighbouring mountains, when the clouds rain down sand till the ground is covered many feet deep, and every particle of vegetation is destroyed. I had an opportunity of observing a cutting made by a stream in this district, and I found traces of three several depositions of volcanic dust, the last as much as thirteen feet deep.

Vegetation advances in Iceland with none of that rapidity with which it covers the flanks of Vesuvius, and sand in Iceland is many hundreds of years old before it becomes covered with a scanty growth of marram and moss campion.

Part of this elevated table-land of desert is studded with countless lakes of all shapes and sizes, disconnected, landlocked; some, quiet tarns of crystal clear water others winding among the hills, ruffled and tossed into

angry waves by the cutting blasts which howl over the waste. This wild region is utterly barren. The hills are bare, exposed stone, broken into angular fragments and torn into gullies by the melting snows of spring. The elevated plains are masses of splintered trap and black mud, into which a horse will flounder to its belly. The dales are occasionally grey with moss, and partially clothed with stunted willow.

But every spring thaw helps to destroy the little amount of vegetation which exists, as the icy water tears down the hill-slopes and rips up the moss, or bears away the sandy soil in which the willow found root.

It must not be thought that a mossy, willowy bottom is common. You may travel all day without coming to one, but a few do exist, known only to certain individuals who haunt the waste during the summer, gathering the *lichen islandicus,* or seeking swans.

This region bears some resemblance to the Siberian tundras, but it is more barren. The tundras are moss-covered, and nourish herds of reindeer; but the *heidis* of the centre of Iceland could not support any quadruped. For the most part this desert is devoid of living creatures, for birds will not frequent spots where there is no vegetation.

Wherever a morass of moss, blaeberry, and willow is to be found, however, multitudes of wild fowl congregate. The lakes teem with red-fleshed Alpine trout and magnificent char, and where the fish are, there are to be found the swan and the diver.

Swans breed in considerable numbers among these lakes, unmolested except by a hardy native who may venture into the wilds to shoot them for their feathers. The swan is of only one species, the *cygnus musicus*: some naturalists have asserted that another species is to be found in the island, but the natives are very positive that one kind only visits the island, and certainly amongst those which I saw, I noticed none but the hoopers. Glorious, indeed, is the note, shrill as a trumpet-call, uttered by this majestic bird, when the labours of incubation are completed, and it sings its pæan of triumph over its fledgelings.

The swans generally are in pairs in a lake: among these tarns it is rare to find more than one couple to each sheet of water. An attempt on the part of a second pair to intrude is resented as an intrusion, the swans regarding the lake as an Englishman regards his house—as a castle. But this is not the case always. I counted some eighteen swans on the great lake in the Vatnsdalr; but there the sheet was extensive. Perhaps the reason of the tenacity of the swans on the *Arnarvatn heidi* to their rights is the scarcity of provender, and they may be aware that what is enough for two would be starving for four.

Another bird frequenting these lakes, also in couples, is the Great Northern Diver, a magnificent fellow in gorgeous metallic glitter of green and black, his wings and back sprinkled with white, and his breast of spotless purity. The size of the bird is great, his neck and head well proportioned, the latter narrow and armed with a pointed dark-coloured bill, and furnished with bright crimson eyes, like rubies.

The diver is a heavy bird, and a clumsy walker; but he flies well, though low, rising when alarmed from his lone dark pool with a weird cry, mingled with gulping whoops, like the laughter of a fiend. The diver is a very powerful swimmer, and it is difficult for a boat to keep

THE GREAT NORTHERN DIVER.

up with him. He laughs at a storm, dancing like a cork on the waters, plunging through the waves and appearing on the other side with a fish in his mouth, which he swallows with a toss of his head.

In the neighbourhood of the lakes where there is vegetation the whimbrel stands on his long legs, uttering his wild sad cry, and seeming quite unconcerned if you present your gun. Have him we must, for we depend entirely for provisions in these wastes on what we shoot; and whimbrel, though stringy and tasteless, is not to be despised when little else is to be got.

Ah! we have disturbed a covey of ptarmigans. They looked like grey stones, crouching so unconcernedly on the ground as we rode by. But the ptarmigan is sure before long to give notice of his presence, for he is proud of his voice, and one might pass within a few feet of the bird without noticing him, but for his tell-tale call—riö, riö, riö—which has given him his name in Iceland of Rjupr.

We catch the zick-zack of the snipe in yon morass, and the ceaseless melancholy pipe of the golden plover sounds from every stony hill around the tarn. Just here there is abundance of life; a gun-shot beyond the top of the rise you will not see or hear a bird. If you are lucky, you will catch sight of the great snowy owl, like a snow-ball, sailing by, uttering its solemn note. Its haunts are somewhere among the unvisited, unknown recesses of the vast Jokülls which close the view on the south.

Here, close to us, is a little snow bunting, sitting wagging its tail and cheeping; lucky bunting that you are! had the owl but seen you, you would not be perched so unconcernedly there. How tame the little being is, or rather how stupid; you have only to steal up softly whilst it is occupied cheeping, and you can catch it in your hand. These rocks around us harbour countless buntings, but their nests are so far in among the crevices that it is a difficult matter to obtain an egg.

Have done with the birds: let us take a glance at the flora of this wild spot. This is scanty. The very moss in some places is turned black as coal by the icy tricklings from the snow, and it is only where there is a dry sheltered spot that any flowers can blossom. There are a few.

The pale blue butterwort, on its sickly leaves, trembles timorously in the piercing blasts which roll over the Jokülls, and yet bravely endures them. I do not think the little flower has as cheerful a hue here as in the south. It seems blanched with cold.

The grass of Parnassus is also to be found, but the little bullet heads are not yet unfolded. On a southern slope of volcanic ash a scanty growth of creeping azalea may be discovered, and a few varieties of heath which I cannot identify just now, as they have not yet flowered.

In the marsh at the head of this tarn, in which my poor ponies are wading after the young willow-tops, I find the bog whortle and the blaeberry, now coming into flower; and I light upon a bunch of *Bartsia alpina*, its rich plum-coloured flowers just beginning to open.

On the lava rocks, especially when old, may be seen masses of pale *Dryas octopetala*—a glorious flower, with its eight delicate milky petals and its sunny eye. Nowhere have I seen this plant in such perfection as in

Iceland; the blossoms are larger there than I have seen in the Alps or the Pyrenees, but probably the volcanic constituents of the rock on which it lives are those best suited for its development.

We may find a few saxifrages also, but one flower, which is sure to attract the eye, is the dwarf campion, of all gradations of colour, from pure snow-white to carmine pink, in dense masses of little blossoms, studding the sand, and growing where nothing else can grow. Brave, bonny little plant! I have become attached to it from association, as it has cheered my eye, wearied with the unrelieved monotony of black wastes for miles and miles in Iceland.

It was impossible to cross this desert in a day, and I was obliged to obtain a guide to direct me to some spot where I could encamp for the night, and where there was sufficient herbage for the support of my ponies. We were in the saddle for the greater part of the day, winding among barren stony hills, traversing rolling swells of exposed trap, trotting over sandy sweeps, skirting bristling barriers of lava, and threading our way among countless sheets of pale milky water, holding snow in solution, and not sufficiently warm to become transparent.

At last, about six o'clock in the evening, we reached a lake about three miles long and a mile wide, on which my guide kept a boat for the purpose of fishing. He led us to a node of rock, covered with moss, at the foot of which was a heap of brushwood, which he had sent

THE DESERT. 33

thither some days before, on the backs of ponies, to serve him as fuel when he came to spend a week in fishing.

LANDSCAPE IN THE DESERT.

Our teeth were chattering with cold, and our whole frames shivering, though we were well on in the summer —within a day or two of the end of June ; we were glad

D

enough accordingly to secure some of **this wood** and to make a fire. We had a couple of tents, and these were soon erected, though we had **considerable** difficulty in obtaining a suitable site, **as the mossy ground** was covered with lumps like enormous mole-hills as **close together as they could stand.** If we left the **immediate** neighbourhood of the rock just mentioned, we found ourselves in a quaking bog; and if we ascended the hill-side, we came upon bare stone on which we could not fix our tents, there being no possibility of driving in the pegs.

And now I must give an idea of the scene from the rise above this **tarn, as viewed at** midnight, **when** I made the sketch.

Imagine, then, the lake, bright as a mirror, reflecting the blue-green of the sky, which was kindled with the beams of the sun, now touching the sea in the north, which is invisible to us as some miles of rolling waste intervene. The middle distance is the Heidi, swell on swell of stone and sand, of a deep umber hue, deepening into black. Just at the lake-edge my little tent stands out a flake of white against the sombre ground. **Ah!** you think there was **moss** where I pitched it. **True**; but the moss on these wastes **is not** green, but ash grey. My little flag, an admiral of the white pennant, charged with a red cross, is the only point **of bright colour** to relieve the monotony of the tints.

Over the last **swell of** the desert, where the umber is becoming purple **with** distance, rises with one start a mighty dome of **ice**, raised on precipitous flanks of trap, black when you are near them, but tinted the sweetest violet in the distance. The mighty pile of snow and ice rises from these abrupt scarps with a gentle curve, undinted to the very summit, looking soft and downy as a swan's breast. As the sun rests on the glittering heap it blushes to the tenderest rose and sparkles like a precious gem. The scene is entrancingly lovely.

Far off behind this Joküll, which by the way is called Eirek's Joküll, stretches another—Lang Joküll—like a thread of white cloud, resting on the horizon, and lost in the distance of the south-east. To our right, Eirek's Joküll throws out a spur of precipitous rock, jauntily capped with snow, and beyond that rises the cone of Strútur, an extinct volcano. To the north-west, as the air is so clear, we can catch sight of the marvellous Baula, a mountain which is considered one of the wonders of Iceland, as it is a perfect cone, running to a point, 3,500 feet high, with so rapid a slope that snow never rests on it.

The great central wilderness is, as I have already stated, almost entirely unexplored. Three "tracks" alone cross it throughout the length of the island, and the country right and left of these tracks is quite unknown.

When I speak of a track, I do not mean a road. Roads there are none in Iceland, no, not even paths. A trackway over a waste is simply formed by piling three or four stones on the top of a rock. This is called a *vardr*. From this point an experienced eye can detect another vardr, perhaps on the horizon. Often I could not see them, but the Icelander has the eye of an eagle, and he detects one immediately.

The horses have then to make the best of their way from one vardr to another, wriggling among stones, floundering into mud-bogs, picking their way among splinters of trap or lava, often making the most compli-

AN "INN" ON THE TRACK.

cated windings to reach a spot on the horizon of a hill which you could strike with an Enfield.

The reason of the country being so unexplored is just this: if you lose your track in these wastes, God help you! you are lost. The compass will not guide you correctly, for the needle does not always act when you are crossing igneous rock. You may wander for days before you reach grass, and if your ponies die you will hardly be able to reach a place of safety on foot.

The Icelanders had, and in some parts have still, a conviction that the recesses of these wilds are inhabited by a race of men of their own stock, but slightly differing from them in their language and in their dress. They call these people Utlegumennir, and there are some curious stories told about them.

They are supposed to be the descendants of outlaws and robbers, who in old times haunted these deserts, and who having discovered fertile valleys in the heart of the wilderness, are content to reside there, and inherit a feeling of enmity against the coast-dwellers, who expelled their ancestors from the community of their fellow-men. These people are said to be sadly deficient in iron, and to shoe their horses with horn. They are thought to have made their appearance occasionally when merchant ships have entered the fiords to trade with the natives.

Of course the existence of this race is a possibility, but I cannot say anything for its probability. When we consider that the population of Iceland is only 68,000, and that it is a third larger than Ireland, and that this population is confined to the coast and to the banks of the rivers just above their entrance into the friths, it leaves ample room for a colony in the heart of the country to live undisturbed.

About two o'clock at night—if I may call it "night" when it is light, the sun just beginning to struggle up the sky again, and Eirek's Joküll still bathed in his beams—we turned into our tents for the night, putting four guides into a little horseman's tent, 5 ft. 6 in. by 3 ft. 6 in., which was close enough packing to keep them warm.

Storm and rain came on, and we had a miserable night, the water pouring over the floor of our tents and soaking all our bedding. We were somewhat aching and rheumatic when we crawled forth the next morning to a breakfast on cold boiled plover and char. But travelling is a succession of pleasures and pain, of comfort and discomfort, of enjoyment and annoyance, and we must take all as it comes.

ICELAND.

CHAPTER III.

THE PÉOPLE.

THERE is no hotel in Iceland, always excepting the miserable pot-house which does duty at the capital. The churches are the hostelries, and the clergy, miserably poor though they be, are the public exponents of a hospitality which is a national virtue. You sleep and eat, and may even smoke at your ease, in the churches. The clergy join you, if you wish it, at such festivity, and frequently the meal, or its choicest portion, is their contribution.

The churches are ridiculously small buildings. The one which formerly stood at Tingvalla—one of the great sights of the island, from being the seat of the old Athling or open-air Parliament—was only twenty-five feet by ten, and when the clergyman was in the pulpit his head was above the rafters! The new church at the place mentioned is on a somewhat larger scale than its predecessor; but many sacred edifices, I was informed, still exist in the island, not larger than the old church referred to. The people are so widely scattered, that it is difficult in stormy weather to fill even these diminutive buildings.

The clergy possess incomes varying generally from 6*l*. to 10*l*. a year, exclusive of a few trifling fees, and they have a house and farm besides. They work at their farms as hard as the meanest of their parishioners; and, as a rule, are not very much elevated above them in intelligence or learning. To this remark, however, there have been, and still are, many notable exceptions.

It is not an uncommon thing for the traveller to find an entertainment set out for his acceptance on the altar of the church in which he resides, and in the dark evenings to have the large candles on the altar lit for his use. We did not stand in need of such aid, as we carried our own tent and commissariat; but for those who trust to church accommodation and clergy entertainers, it is a common, but at first a somewhat startling, event.

The Icelanders are Lutherans, and very strict, and they are somewhat bigoted. I believe that there is one solitary Romanist in the island, and for his benefit, as well as for the good of the French fishermen who annually frequent the coast for a few months, there are two Roman Catholic priests at Reykjavik all the year round, and a very agreeable gentleman whom we met, and who is designated by the ambitious title of "Préfet Apostolique du Pôle Nord," visits them yearly to see that their duty is rightly performed.

The mode of travelling in Iceland is somewhat eccentric and not a little fatiguing. The ground is so encumbered with masses of stone, and the distances from place to place so great, that a pedestrian has no chance; and

TRAVELLING IN ICELAND.

as railways and even highways are unknown, the shortlimbed, big-headed, shaggy, intelligent pony of the country is made to carry everybody and everything that requires transport. There are some seventy thousand of these most useful animals on the island, and their surefootedness is such that the traveller soon learns to dash at full speed, like a native, across ground bristling with countless stones that razor-like project from the surface, ready to mutilate him grievously if he fall upon them.

The only roads are mere tracks, under two feet broad, made by the various generations of ponies, and left entirely to the care of snow-drift and glacier. These, partly covered with stones, wind zig-zag between the greater rock-masses, and ford innumerable bridgeless rivers, that in short but fierce courses roll down "pale from the glaciers" to lake or sea. Wherever there is soil the path eats its way into the ground, and thus a high turf bank stands up on either side, thickly studded with rough stones; and in avoiding contact with such fracturing and dislocating agencies, feats of horsemanship have to be performed which leave most unpleasant impressions on bone and muscle when repose is sought after your ten hours' scamper.

The ponies are so diminutive, and the traveller is generally so enveloped in coats, plaids, and capes, that the moving mass appears at a little distance all man and no pony. When things look ugly, the only alternative is to shut the eyes and hold the breath, and if the reins are left loose, your intelligent bearer will soon extricate you from all difficulty.

Each traveller has two ponies for his own use, and two for each guide and load of baggage, so that the number of animals accompanying even a small party is very considerable. The relays are driven by lash and cry, in a wild surging wave before; and as the flying column winds round the shoulder of a mountain, or flits like a cloud across valleys where no other living thing is seen, a momentary life and animation is imparted to scenes otherwise often singularly unattractive.

Except potatoes, and a few other hardy vegetables, no crops come to maturity in Iceland, and corn is never sown. Truly

"No products here the barren hills afford,
But man and steel—the soldier and his sword."

The sea is the Icelander's great storehouse. From it he obtains the chief staple of his diet and the main item of his export. Providence has, in the seething shoals of every species of fish which frequent these seas, compensated in a great measure for the sterility of the land. A few hours, in the proper season, suffices to fill a boat with magnificent fish, and the whole population, men, women, and children, abjectly worship the cod, who is *here* undisputed king.

Every house near the coast is redolent of cod. The eaves are festooned with their bodies, the doorways are straitened by them, the children cut their teeth on them, and the very ponies love and eat them. Stacks—veritable stacks of cod, roped and thatched like peats in Scotland—meet you by the highways, and ships freighted with them sail for the delectation of Catholic countries. These Icelanders are the veritable Ichthyophagi. It is only after seeing a native develop the hidden mysteries of a cod's head that you become aware of how much

"curious eating" it affords. Many boat-loads of co
from these distant seas find their way to the Londo
market, whose wealth attracts the products of the whol
known world.

INTERIOR OF A HOUSE.

If Mr. Cod was aware of what an interest the Icelande
has in his welfare, I doubt not he would feel deepl
gratified. He little thinks, as he rubs his cold nose o

the tangle, and gazes with his glassy unimaginative eye at the inviting bait, how many firesides up-stairs are rendered warm at the expense of himself and his relations.

Besides fish, the Icelander feeds on milk-curd (similar to that used by the Arabs and Kaffirs), occasionally rye-bread and mutton, and, on rare occasions, potatoes, and even coffee. Notwithstanding their unvaried and not very wholesome diet, the Icelanders are large, strong, flaxen-haired, and healthy-looking men. Their houses cannot certainly contribute to their healthfulness, as they are built apparently with the sole object of excluding light and air, and imprisoning every fetid effluvium.

Violent epidemics, very similar in their nature and malignancy to those which devastated our own country during the Middle Ages, have, within recent times, swept over the land; and now leprosy, such as is seen throughout the East, is a common disease. As the whole population of the island is below 70,000, an epidemic produces a most terrible effect on the native society.

There are no tradesmen, properly so called, in Iceland, and there are no village schools. The distances between the farms make both impossible. "In the nights of winter," however, "when the cold north winds blow and the long howling of the wolves is heard amidst the snow," the farmer acts in turn the part of tailor, shoemaker, smith, and carpenter, and so carefully instructs his children, that the whole population are said to be very efficiently educated.

The Icelanders are true Scandinavians of the unmixed *sangre-bleu*. They speak the pure Norse, from which some 60 per cent. of our own language is derived. In their honesty, truthfulness, hospitality, maritime enterprise, courage, and humble piety, we British are fain to trace some of our most cherished national traits, and from them undoubtedly we obtained our ideas of representative parliaments, trial by jury, and other honoured institutions.

In manners, the Icelanders are quiet, subdued, and contented. Music and dancing are said to be almost unknown; we certainly saw no evidence of either art being practised. The long, dawnless winter nights, when the sun is replaced by the pale reflection of the stars from snow and ice, or the flashing coruscations of the Aurora wandering from horizon to zenith in brilliant tints of evanescent glory, must give a complexion to the thoughts and dispositions as it moulds the habits and occupations of men.

So frigid and inhospitable a climate must cramp the conception and harden the temperament. How different are the external influences which surround the Icelander from those affecting the Italian, Egyptian, or Indian! And yet that the grand scenes of the North are well fitted to fire the imagination, and develop the more thoughtful faculties, is well evinced in the Eddas and Sagas of the many Icelandic writers. It is now well understood that not a few of those wild, fanciful German legends which we value so much, are but translations of Icelandic tales ; and we know that histories and poems were written in Iceland long before we, in Great Britian, had emerged from barbarism.

Much of the domestic history of Iceland is an account of contests waged with physical evils ; and when we thus see men successfully contending with storm and pestilence, with volcanos and earthquakes, with long seasons of darkness, with snow and ice, with a land "whose stones are iron, and whose hills are brass," almost cut off from intercourse with other nations, and having but few natural resources on which to fall back, we cannot but award them our highest admiration and respect.

Their love of country is proverbial, notwithstanding "the small mercies" for which they have to be thankful. So true is it that—

> " The shuddering tenant of the Frigid Zone
> Boldly proclaims that happiest spot his own,
> Extols the treasures of his stormy seas,
> And his long nights of revelry and ease ;
> So the loud torrent, and the whirlwind's roar,
> But bind him to his native mountains more."

The discomfort of a residence in Iceland is much enhanced by the want of fuel. The springs of hot water would be most providential institutions in such a land if the inhabitants turned them to economic uses. There are no trees, unless the pigmy willows and birch, some few inches high, which are found in a few spots, and ambitiously called "forests," are to be so designated. There is little or no turf also; yet there is no lack of wood, though no ship or human hand brings it to their shores.

The Gulf-Stream sweeps part of the coast, assuaging in a most notable degree the severity of their climate. It also bears to them, from the long circuit of its stately march, innumerable trees of many species with roots and branches attached, and logs of valuable wood, gnawed by the sea, to brighten the hearth and build their log houses firm against the storm.

Game is very plentiful in Iceland. With salmon and sea-trout in the streams, and teal, snipe, golden plover, ptarmigan, wild goose, and wild swan on the fiörds and moors, the sportsman need never be at a loss; not to speak of the countless flocks of sea-birds which frequent the coast, from the "Great Northern Diver" to the little fat puffin, which only needs to be shorn of its feathers, have a wick passed through his body, and be set on end in a saucer, in order to form a brilliant light for the household.

Besides fish, there are exported from Iceland, wool, eider-down feathers, knitted things in great numbers, and sulphur. The whole public annual income of the island is but 3,000*l*., and the Government expends fully twice that sum upon it, so that the connection is not a very profitable one for the mother country.

I would add that of the many natural beauties of the

BIRD-CATCHING.

country, **none struck me more** than the wonderfully diversified shape and colour of the mountains.

Some are sharp, like needles, others form regular cones, others stand out in **long splintered** ridges, "**bitten into barrenness by the hunger of the** north wind," or tormented **into great rough masses of** tumbled rock, and so present **an** infinite variety **of** beautiful objects **in** the landscape.

The colouring, too, especially **in the morning and evening, is really extraordinary.** Not **only are the** varieties of shade **great, but they are most brilliant and intense:** deep **brown and black, relieved by many degrees of green and grey, with** dashes **of purple,** orange, **and even rose and red.** These, combined for the most part **in the most** harmonious hues, and reflected **by** an **atmosphere of the most dazzling** clearness, far surpass **the artist's power of** imitation.

Some of the mountain masses rise dark and desolate without **soil or trace of vegetation. They look** like great beams **of iron** binding the land together. Others **spring,** a glorious **glittering pyramid of snow and ice, from** the blue sea **or the green** grassy plain. **Yet, with** all this— and **we** intensely enjoyed **it—how inexpressibly we** admired **our own dear land, when, after seeing so much** barren **sterility, we found ourselves travelling through the** harvest fields **of Aberdeenshire, and saw "the swathes of its corn glowing and burning from** field **to** field," **and** looked into the peaceful homesteads **and** orchards, **full to** overflowing with the generous fruits of the earth, **and saw**

again the " bosky knowes," brilliant with purple heather, rise up amidst glades of tangled wild flowers and soft-creeping moss! Truly it seemed "a generous land, gilded with corn, and fragrant with deep grass; bright with capricious plenty, and laughing from vale to vale in fitful fulness kind and wild."

NORTHERN· RUSSIA.

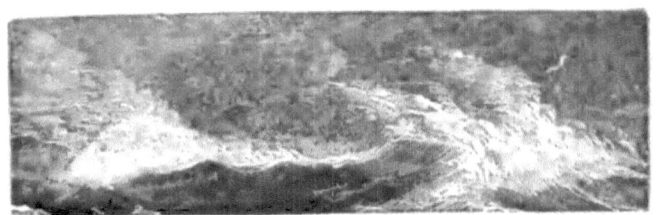

NORTHERN RUSSIA.

CHAPTER I.

THROUGH THE BALTIC.

I HAVE little to say about it. The fact is that almost all voyages out of sight of land are much the same.

In every ship there is the same sort of steward and passengers; the same bustle for berths at starting; the same running about through the cabin and on deck, with hat-boxes, carpet-bags, and new portmanteaus, getting settled down.

The same smells too!—blame me not for dwelling on them—most notable facts are they, inasmuch as the nose conveys to the soul fully as much information regarding the external world as any other of the senses. Hence there is a seashore smell; a highland moor smell; a coach smell; a first, second, and third class smell; a church smell; "a subtle smell which spring unbinds," as

Wordsworth well knew, having had the advantage of a large poetic nose to perceive it. No man feels himself abroad until he has inhaled the smell of the "salle à manger" or the "Speise Saal." And thus no man realizes that he is at sea until he has felt the smell of the cabin, and of those submarine cells called state-rooms— an aroma which stands alone, a product of sea and land, yet nothing else on sea or land having a scent like it!

Then there are much about the same kind of waves on every sea, that is to say, on ordinary occasions; for when put to it by a gale of wind, I would back the Atlantic, anywhere between Cape Race and Cape Clear, against all the treasures of the great deep, for breaking, topping, sweeping, roaring blue seas. The North Sea is not, indeed, to be despised, especially when it fights with the winds, as Duncan did with the Dutch over the Dogger-bank; but the Baltic, though ambitious, and often seriously angry, has all the testiness of a fresh-water lake, but wants the grand majesty, the mountain-swing of the real old Ocean. It is fierce and furious, not awful and overwhelming like the Atlantic.

Our passengers were, of course, divided between the whole and the sick, with various species under this last genus, from those possessing a solemn gravity and pensive meditativeness, down to a solitary inert mass of helpless agony, unconscious apparently of every existence except that of the steward, whose name was feebly uttered, by day and night, in spasmodic intervals. I have ever had the good fortune to be among the whole and hearty.

Our good ship, I may add, was the *Admiral*, sailing from Hull; and our good captain, than whom a worthier

FISHING-SMACK.

man or more experienced sailor sails not the sea, was Brown.

We took seven days to St. Petersburg. Remember that fact ere ye thoughtlessly venture to peep into Russia. The most interesting spectacle on the North Sea was fishing-smacks. We passed several out of sight of land. They trawl over those endless banks for months, consigning their cargoes from time to time to vessels which convey them to British or continental markets, but the same crew always remaining in the smack. There they lie, pitching and tossing, reefing and tacking, hauling and trawling, lying to and bearing away, night and day, through mist, and spit, and salt sea-foam, with wet nets, wet fish, wet sails, wet ropes, wet clothes, wet skies!

How cosy and comfortable is any returned convict, or inhabitant of one of our well-regulated prisons, compared with these poor fellows! We would recommend "Four months' fishing on the North Sea," as a sentence to be passed upon all those genteel criminals who would miss the theatre and comfortable tavern. It would cool their passions, improve their health, cultivate their good habits, or kill them.

After three days, we saw in the distant horizon a few specks, and were told that they represented Jutland; then, by-and-by, came the Olman light; then, some ten hours after, the Skagen lighthouse, marking a low line of sands, on which we counted five old wrecks; then, twelve hours farther, with occasional peeps of misty streaks which were called dry land, the hitherto almost unseen shores began to come nearer. In a few hours we could see corn-fields, and trees, and then houses, both on the Swedish and Danish coast, but no scenery worth remarking, until at last, right ahead, at some distance, we saw a large square building, which we were told was the Castle of Kronberg, by Elsineur.

We anchored for an hour at Elsineur to take in a pilot; and landed in honour of Hamlet.

I saw nothing very noticeable about this classic spot,

ELSINEUR.

except excellent cherries and some good cherry cordial; also two tug-boats, representing the genius and the influence of Shakspere in this harbour of prose—the one being called Hamlet, and the other Ophelia! We were surprised at finding Elsineur neither "wild," "stormy," nor "steep," but a quiet little wooden town, full of fish and sailors; with its old castle, half a mile off, rising from the very margin of the sea, and wearing the look more of a decayed palace than of a warlike fortress. One would think from its appearance that it is fit for little more than firing royal salutes.

A few hours after passing Elsineur, the sea widens out again until Copenhagen is reached, sweeping round the margin of an ample bay. The day we first saw it was lovely, the sea a dead calm, and the waters alive with vessels. Various buildings were pointed out as we leisurely surveyed the city while landing our pilot; but I saw only the two batteries before which the British fleet poured their broadsides, sixty years ago, for three hours, during the hottest fight ever witnessed by Nelson; and I also saw more clearly than these the little man himself, putting the telescope to his blind eye, and turning it through the smoke towards Parker and his No. 39 signal, ordering the hero to withdraw his ships from the terrific combat. I need only say, that every man of us got up his "Nelson and the North," to the best of his ability, and with becoming patriotism.

Away we went out of the Cattegat and up the Baltic, passing the long island of Gothland, flat and shaped like a tombstone seen sideways;—on, across the Gulf of Bothnia, with sunsets of surpassing glory, and skies red and fiery from the west up to the zenith, and down to the eastern horizon, which glowed as if with sunrise;—on we went, rolling and pitching away with a quarter wind, and all sail set, the right paddle now buried in the sea, and apparently dying of suffocation, the steam giving a wheezing groan as if in sympathy, then, after a roll to port, lightly capping the top of the foaming billows, while the opposite paddle was struggling for existence; the persevering and strong engine all the while doing its duty with an air of dignified respectability, but greatly wanting in zeal;—on, passing the time with the usual routine of meals and conversation, enlivened by the screams of two pigs who paraded the main-deck, and received daily a powerful scrubbing from the sailors, while a sheep, tawny with coal dust, contemplated the scene in peace;—on we went, with a fresh breeze and broken sea, passing several cold and dreary lighthouses and lightships, until, one morning, we were told that a few scratches on the horizon were Cronstadt.

Then came Sir Charles Napier's farthest point of observation, Tamboukin lighthouse, until, finally, we bravely advanced towards the dreaded forts, which did not presume to stop our progress, until we blew off our steam, and anchored close to the pier in the busy harbour. So ended our voyage.

Before getting into the little steamer which conveys us to St. Petersburg, twenty miles up "the firth," let me tell you a short adventure of one of the passengers, the Russian Lieutenant K—y, who left us at Cronstadt. The story has been told before, but I will tell it in as nearly as possible the words of the Lieutenant, and as I took it down at the time in my note-book. I may add that, like most educated Russians, the Lieutenant spoke excellent English.

"The *Diana* frigate, of which I was an officer, was commanded by Admiral Pontaveen. We anchored on the 23rd of December 1855, in the harbour of Sinoda, in Japan. We had on board about 500 of a crew. About half-past nine in the morning we were surprised to see the boats afloat which we had sent on shore, and which had been all drawn up on the beach. But, immediately, our surprise was still greater, in seeing wooden houses floating past us!

"We guessed at once that an earthquake beneath and around us was taking place. Our conjectures were, alas! too true. It proved to be a very fearful earthquake, and continued for seven hours, or until half-past four in the afternoon. During this dreadful time our frigate was swept out of and into the bay by the sea. Anchors were of no use, for land and sea were changing places. We were now on the ground, and the next moment afloat, and again on shore, swinging back and forward, guns breaking loose, killing some, and terrifying all. Our keel was torn off and our rudder lost. At last we were suddenly swept up from the outer bay into an inner harbour. Having reached it, we were seized by the waves as by a whirlpool, and the frigate spinned round and round *forty-five times in thirty minutes!*

"It was awful, more especially as nothing whatever could be done to save us. No one could guess what the next minute would bring forth. We were, of course, unable to save a single life of the poor people, except that of an old woman whom we seized as she was sweeping past us on the roof of her wooden house.

"After the earthquake ceased, we found the ship leaking so much that we landed all her guns as speedily as possible, wrapped a sail round her to try and stop the leak, and then in our miserably disabled state endeavoured to navigate her to a harbour not far off where we could refit. But our misfortunes were not ended!

"We had no sooner entered the open sea than a violent gale arose, and at night too. All now seemed over with us and our poor ship. We tried to hold her fast, or at least check her way, by dropping two anchors. But early in the morning we descried, about a cable's length to leeward, a wild and rocky coast, up whose steep precipices the sea was dashing its spray. One small nook of white sand, among the rocks, was at last seen.

"A boat was sent on shore with a rope; its crew managed to land and to fasten it. By this means we got the rest of the crew on shore, at first, by tying round each man a line which was conveyed to the party on shore, who hauled him to land, half drowned, through the surf. But we improved upon this by anchoring a boat immediately outside the breakers, and thus the drag through the water was shorter. Thus every man of our 500 got on shore in safety.

"Next day the gale ceased, and the frigate, to our surprise, still rode at her anchors. Was it possible yet to save the good ship? It was resolved to make the attempt. We were able to collect very speedily 100 Japanese junks to tow her into a safe harbour. The junks were all made fast, the ship's anchors raised, and away they rowed, towing her, when, suddenly, down she went, head foremost, to the bottom, like a stone! Well, we all went on shore again, and I must here say, that from first to last we were most kindly treated by the Japanese. Our numbers may possibly have awed them; but it is but fair to give them all credit for what they did, and did so well.

"What now was to be done? We resolved at once to build a schooner. Everything had to be extemporized, but so heartily did we work, that from the time we cut down the first tree to build our craft, until she was afloat, was only four months. The admiral (as noble a fellow as ever lived, and, by the way, married to an English lady, which, of course, accounts for his excellence!) set sail with as many of the crew as he could stow away, for the river Amoor, distant about 1,300 miles. In her voyage, the schooner was obliged to pass through the British Fleet. So little idea had good John Bull that a Russian admiral was near him, that, on perceiving the approach of the unknown vessel, supposing, of course, that in those distant seas she was one of their own, he even showed a light, while another ship hailed her to 'keep off.' The admiral was ready to throw his valuable charts and also his despatches overboard, had he been taken. But he escaped into the 'Amoor.'

"The next division of the shipwrecked crew chartered an American ship, and escaped the British. The third and last division, of which I was one, tried to escape, but were captured by the British man of war the *Baraccoota*. I remained a prisoner of war for about a year, visiting various ports in India, and I was treated with such courtesy and kindness that, to tell the truth, I would have no objections to be again taken prisoner by a ship of the British navy! At all events, I shall never forget my generous friends and the *Baraccoota*." Such was the story of the Russian lieutenant.

NORTHERN RUSSIA.

CHAPTER II.

CRONSTADT.

THERE is nothing very imposing about Cronstadt—I mean in the sense in which Gibraltar, or Quebec, or any such mountain fortresses are imposing. But to a skilled eye the soldier lying on the ground behind a bush with an Enfield rifle, is much more awing than a huge Goliath with his spear boastfully challenging the armies of Israel; and so these forts, built on low islands, or rising out of the water like three-storied cotton-factories, have a firm, dogged, business look about them. They are evidently built for guns, and for nothing else, to knock down everything, and to defy anything to return the compliment.

And so with great respect we first passed Fort Alexander, rising out of the sea on our left, and Peter Vahki on an island to the right (a narrow channel intervening),

CRONSTADT. 67

with the Risbank between it and the opposite shore; and then with a respect increasing with the forts and their number of guns, we sailed past Fort Constantine backing Alexander, and Fort Menschikoff in the rear of all.

It is quite evident that no fleet, unless cased in iron, could run the gauntlet, first *between* Alexander and Peter Vahki, and then past Constantine and Menschikoff, with hundreds of guns on the shore supporting them. But no one doubts the certainty of their destruction during the war, had Sir Charles Napier attacked the island of Cronstadt from the rear. But the water was too shallow for anything but gun and mortar boats, and of course there were none provided, until the Czar had time to make any attempt in the rear impracticable.

It is not difficult to understand the relative positions of Cronstadt and St. Petersburg. The Neva empties its waters into a shallow firth about twenty miles long and, as far as I remember, two or three miles broad. The entrance of the firth is guarded by the island and docks of Cronstadt, which is connected with the opposite shore to our right in going to the capital by two small fortified islands. The water is too shallow to admit of any vessels, but those of a light draught, reaching the anchorage at Cronstadt (except by one passage close to the forts), or of going beyond that point to St Petersburg, which is twenty miles up the firth.

The port of Cronstadt is therefore a busy place, with all sorts and sizes of shipping in its docks, and a goodly array of ships of war lying side by side, with their rigging down, in the navy dock, and looking by no means imposing.

The confusion for more than an hour at Cronstadt, after we were moored near the wharf, and before we got ourselves and our baggage transferred to the small steamer which conveyed us to St. Petersburg, cannot be described. The grey-coated and large-booted men who came on board from the custom-house, seemed portraits from the *Illustrated News* of the Crimean Russian soldiers come alive.

Once they were on board, there arose such a medley of sounds from the roar of steam; the Babel of Russian; the rushing to and fro with papers; the meeting of friends; the searching for luggage; the affectionate kisses between Russian men and old friends among our passengers; the roaring out questions and answers by everybody; and everybody apparently frantic with haste, or some mysterious burthen, that it was an immense relief when the steam of our small vessel was choked in the boiler, and with rapid paddle we skimmed through the shipping, and between long poles which marked the passage, and were off for the capital. To the right, along the wooded bank, we could discern white houses thickly scattered, and we heard that this was the fashionable summer retreat of the citizens who could afford a country cottage. The left-hand shore is low, wooded, and without the slightest interest.

As we rapidly approached St. Petersburg, one of the most magnificent rainbows I ever beheld spanned the sky

before us from horizon to horizon. Behind us was another resplendent sunset, with the mighty orb like a globe of molten gold, slowly descending amidst gorgeous colours of amethyst, emerald, and gold, until a single star of light rested for a moment, like a glittering diamond on a cushion of gleaming ruby, and then disappeared, while we held our breath with wonder, and a hundred suns then danced before our eyes. Already were the gilt domes of St. Isaac's Church and of the Admiralty reflecting the last rays of evening above a low fringe of forest.

In about two hours after leaving Cronstadt, on our taking a sudden turn to the left, we entered the Neva.

When made fast to the landing-wharf on the shores of the Neva, and before the custom-house, the first thing unquestionably which strikes one as new and quite Russian, that is to say, like what we have heard of Russia from our picture-books, are the droskies—they are thoroughly national, and long may they continue so!

The drosky is a low four-wheel, with two seats supported by old-fashioned, hanging leather springs that make large semicircles behind. The one seat behind is for the driven, a small one above his knees before for the driver. Two persons of small bulk can cram themselves into the seat, but if one of the occupants happens to be a "portly man i' faith," he or his neighbour must suffer grievously.

Every driver or *Vostick* is dressed in exactly the same national costume—the large blue dressing-gown, or kaftan, reaching to the boots, and tied round the waist with a sash, while a low-crowned black felt hat and turned-up brim covers a head, the back of which has thick reddish-brown hair, arrested by the scissors as it touches the coat, while the front is adorned by a face with cocked nose, large mouth, and a general dusty, turnipy, and, on the whole, stolidly kind expression.

There is a myth about shepherds being able to distinguish one sheep from another by the expression of their countenances. We don't believe James Hogg himself, after marking the idiosyncrasies of all the black or white faces on Ettrick, would ever be able to discover the difference between one *Vostick* (Isvostchik) and another.

When the traveller, for the first time, hazards his person in one of those small droskies, and his driver securing a rein in each hand, sets off with rapid speed along the quays and streets of St. Petersburg, he has entered on a new experience in locomotion, unless he has had some personal knowledge, as I have had, of the corduroy roads of America.

Those streets, those memorable streets, surely leave impressions never to be obliterated. They are all paved with small stones, and seldom level, but descending in the centre, along which is an open water-course. But the holes in that pavement! the roughness of those stones! the rattle, plunges, knocks endured! while following a swift-trotting horse and remorseless *Vostick* in a drosky, forms an element of sight-seeing in hot weather which every traveller should carefully consider before he leaves home. Every bone, thew, muscle, and sinew of his frame must be in perfect order to undergo this ordeal.

Rascally-looking Cossack police on their small horses and with their long spears, galloped past; Greek priests with their black robes and broad-brimmed hats, and hair down their back, moved along; and various other types

A VOSTICK.   A BEGGAR.   A PRIEST.

of humanity never seen before. But the eye feebly took in the panorama of a new country. The whole soul was concentrated on the bones of the body, and all natural emotions of gratitude for our safe arrival, and wonder at finding one's-self in Russia, began to dawn only when the drosky was left with a bound of delighted deliverance, as it stopped at **Dom** Felinson's Anglitzke, Nabroshne (so the words sounded to me), which meant, **as I afterwards learned, Miss** Benson's English **Quay,** being the comfortable *pension* to which we were recommended, and into which we gladly entered.

NORTHERN RUSSIA.

CHAPTER III.

ST. PETERSBURG.

SIGHT-SEEING in a new country is a necessity, a doom: the city must be "done." Yet I maintain that it is a serious bore to do it in hot weather, and such weather we experienced in Russia—when the air was at what seemed the boiling-point, with the pavement like a furnace, not a cloud in the sky, and the sun fierce and intolerable.

Where is the man who, in such circumstances, has not felt a nervous shiver, in spite of all his curiosity, as he stood at the hotel door, "Murray" in hand, about to pace it till dinner time through palaces, museums, churches, streets, and squares? After all is finished with a late dinner, the irresistible doom still remains to spend the evening at Tivoli, the "gardens," or some of those places attached to every continental city, with crowds of people, coloured lamps, bands of music, chairs in the open air, waiters rushing to and fro with white aprons, and serving coffee, ices, or anything to refresh the languid nerves, or cool the parched throat; but all this must be " done," there is no help for it.

" Why did you come abroad unless to see all that was to be seen ? " asks the new traveller, up to anything.

It is possible, however, slightly to mitigate this heavy, imperious duty.

Beware, first of all, of an enthusiastic, able-bodied, patient, determined sight-seer, who desires to obtain accurate information about everything, who is always discovering national peculiarities—" things one never sees at home "—who takes notes, asks innumerable questions, replies to which no memory can retain were it desirable to do so, and who insists on seeing everything in the museum down to the last Emperor's stocking, or in the palaces down to the Emperor's kitchen. Neither body nor spirit of ordinary mould can stand him this amount of excessive culture.

Then again, if possible, never take a guide. Yet how seldom is it possible to get quit of that attached incubus with shabby-genteel surtout, gloves, and polished old hat. Who on going abroad ever thinks of the trials that await him with " commissionaires " or " valets de place !" Can any man recall the architectural glories of the famous old continental towns, without the presence of a "commissionaire," mingling itself in memory with the beautiful, like a patch on a royal robe.

After considerable experience, we advise the solitary stroll through the town ; the discovery of sights for one's-self; the enjoyment of freedom ; the delight of calm, undisturbed observation ; the power to gaze into shop windows without being waited for, or of sitting alone in a cathedral, without an arm and finger of a guide compelling your eyes to follow their directions. Only be assured that everywhere human beings may be found who will tell you all you wish to know, in every place where you wish to wander, and where you seek to feel rather than to know.

The language, alas ! *that* in Russia is a fearful demand. French and German go far, but when Russ is required, you must get Mr. Schaff to accompany you. But let this be the last resource of desperation. Fortunately for us, we had a perfect guide in one of our travelling companions who knew Russia and the Russians.

Now, I will not trouble my readers by dragging them after me through all the sights of St. Petersburg and Moscow ; this would be almost as bad as driving through their streets in a drosky. Let me just give an abridged catalogue of the chief things which I saw.

In St. Petersburg I visited the principal churches, specially St. Isaac's, great in granite, magnificent in malachite, and hoary in nothing save superstition ; with the Kazan church draped with innumerable banners taken in war—never did an English flag form a part in any such collections!—with keys of many fortresses, and the baton of Davoust, dropped in his cold race from Moscow to Paris.

I saw in these churches the most august services of the Greek communion, getting my pocket picked at the most solemn of them.

I paced through the Winter Palace, from room to room, from bedroom to bedroom, saw all the glories of lapis-lazuli and crown jewels; I revelled among the very beautiful and choice pictures of the Hermitage, one fine building at least; the citadel, with its mint, was not neglected; and I stood among the tombs of the Romanoffs—beside the sleeping body of Peter the Great, great in stature, in resolution, in genius, in whim, in war, in shipbuilding, in city-building, and wood-turning; the tombs also of Paul, the madman and murdered; of Catherine, great in genius and in crime; Alexander, the hero of the great war, overcome by the talk of Napoleon on the Niemen raft, and paying him back at the old Kremlin; and last of all, the tomb of Nicholas, the grand despot, who died of his wounds in the Crimea.

Ah! it was sad to see, as I entered that church, the widow of Nicholas coming out of it, old, infirm, tottering, and agonized by cancer, taking her last look where her once mighty " Czar of all the Russias " lay cold and senseless as a stone, and where she has since joined him. Oh, sickness, pain, and death! what republican levellers are these of us all, and how they unite us more than

ON THE NEVA IN WINTER.

armies or fleets can do, by the tender bonds of sympathy and pitying love!

I need not say that I wandered through the busy streets, paused before the Admiralty, admiring the noble Alexander column, and the long vista of the Nevski Prospect, and stood beside the statue of Peter the Great, whose chief interest to me was the memory of its picture at the corner of an old school atlas; and I *drove* (that cannot be forgotten!) to the monastery of St. Alexander Nevski, and also through the wild islands, the finest park I have ever seen near a great city, rejoicing in the woods and in the flashing streams of the noble Nevas that sweep through the Delta.

We visited all or several of the islands—Kammenoi, Yelaginskoi, Yelagin, Krestorski, Vassali Ostroff, Petrosky, Aptekarskoi, &c., pausing, as the wont is in the evening, to see the glorious sunset from the nearest point to the Baltic; and I wandered through the best sight of all to study Russia and mankind, the Bazaars, the Gos tinnoi Dvor, the Appraxin Rinok, and Tshukin Dvor— those worlds of everything bought or sold in Russia by tens of thousands of dealers; and I paced down the Nevski Prospect more than once; and I visited the museum, and actually saw, not only the skeleton, but the skin and hair of a brute, known to all schoolboys as the Siberian mammoth, which trod the earth, ate, slept, grew old and stupid, and finally died, before Adam was born!

Is the reader wearied of this catalogue?

Yet I am not half done, for I also went twenty miles in one direction to see the Royal Palace of Tzarskoi Selo, built by Peter the Great, with its amber room, its museum full of every species of arms from every nation that ever fought, where the Duke of Wellington's sword and Kos-

THE MAMMOTH.

ciusko's sleep together as harmless as two primroses; and in the grounds of which is the summer-house where that old randy, Catherine, used to entertain company round a table so constructed that every plate descended by machinery to the kitchen, was filled and returned, without the necessity of any servant entering the **room**, which was a great advantage to the morals of the servants; and finally—for this sight-seeing **puts one out of breath**—I visited another palace on **the** left shore **of the firth going to** Cronstadt, called Peterhoff, built **by the half-mad Czar Peter, in which is still** shown his bed, and **dirty flannel** night-cap lying **on** his pillow; **and** another **palace in** the same place, **where the** royal family reside in summer, which has grounds with **no end of splendid** *jets-d'eau*, bands **of** music, Circassian **guards, and** fine soldiers.

This was a small portion of St. **Petersburg** sight-seeing without a word of Alexandrofski and old General Wilson; and besides these, all **Moscow is** before **us yet,** and Moscow **has** its Kremlin, worth **all** St. Petersburg **put together.**

But **before we** part for the present, please, **reader, take in fancy a** chair with me on the balcony, entered from the dining-room, **on** the second story of Miss Benson's excellent boarding-house.

The **guests** who **are seated beside** me and in **the room are** all English, with one exception, **who** shall **be mentioned.** Almost all of them **are** commercial **men. Two or three of them** with unrevealed names **are** probably not so. They maintain **the usual silence and** reserve of Englishmen on **their travels; talk** among themselves, and gaze around **them with** eyes educated **to express a** vacant stare. **Yet these** are very likely **fine fellows, if you only** knew **them.** They have travelled **before now,** have just come from a fishing tour in Norway, have "done" Sweden, Finland, and intend visiting the great fair of Novgorod. They study to appear unconscious of the presence of any other human being in the room, and it is to be presumed that "you must love them, ere you know that they are worthy of your love." Pray don't trouble them, and they won't trouble you. Yet, ten to one the ice will be broken between you, if you are not intrusive, and you will find Jones and Robinson right good fellows.

Sitting in the corner of the balcony, slowly whiffing his cigar, is a British naval officer who has been for many months in St. Petersburg. He was one of the commissioners for arranging the boundary between Turkey and Persia. He, too, is silent and reserved, though an Irishman; but only draw him out, and you will soon discover what a mine of inexhaustible information there is in him, and what sly, *pawky* humour.

What part of the earth does he not know? He will tell you the soundings of every mile in the Gulf of Mexico; and there is hardly a spot from Labrador to New Zealand which does not suggest a story. For years he has wandered with the Arabs of the Desert, from Bagdad to the ruins of Babylon. The Sheiks Hassim and Selim, and every vagabond who wanders over Mesopotamia, are his familiars. No one, except perhaps "Hakim Ross," the famous Scotch doctor of Bagdad, knew them better. A most agreeable companion is the captain.

Gliding in on noiseless tread is an **old** Russian man of **science.** He dines daily at this **table.** Why, no one knows, **for the English** alone frequent it. "The Professor" **is upwards of** seventy, but is still **hale and active. What has he** not seen? Whom does he **not know? What scientific** meeting of *savans* was ever held **in Europe** without "**our** distinguished friend from St. Petersburg" being among them? What invention of any great importance was **ever patented, that the** inventor did not find a card and letter of introduction presented by "Professor ——" from St. Petersburg? Is the *Great Eastern* commenced, finished, **launched—the** Professor **is** there at **each** of these **moments of her** existence. **Is the** Transatlantic telegraph laid? He is the first **at** Valentia, **and the** last to leave. "Please **transmit the** names **of** the Royal Family **of Russia,"** he whispers **to** the **clerks.** He is sure to **receive one of** the **first messages** transmitted, **and** shows it to the **Emperor.**

Oh, how simple he is — a child — mere scientific curiosity; **but is he not** wide awake! He knows far **more of persons** and things in every part of Great **Britain** than **any** inhabitant **of the nation does.** Yet **ask that man one** question about **Russia—try, if you can, and** screw **one ounce of information out of** him — interrogate him about serfage, the political liberty, **or** any **other** question—oh, what ignorance seizes **him! How defective his** memory becomes! He **does not** know; **he does not** remember. He regrets to be unable to inform you. He has indeed no information on such points! Most amiable, accomplished, and learned, yet ignorant professor! I mention him merely as a type of a large class of Russians. Their rule is "get" (never "give") all thou canst.

> " High Heaven rejects the lore,
> Of nicely calculated less or more."

No wonder such persons should be considered "spies." If we conclude that they are not, no thanks to them for so favourable a judgment. But look abroad!

Below is the street, with a drosky-stand, bounded fifty feet across by the granite quay, and beyond, the Neva flowing past, broad, deep, and swift. There are no vessels so high up, except a steamer or two on the opposite wharf.

"What a stupid, dull place," exclaims the naval officer; "how I hate it!"

"And I."

"Ditto, ditto," exclaim others.

"Please give me a light for my cigar," asks a commercial man of his neighbour, "I am dying of *ennui*."

"What a glorious evening! What a sunset! Only look!" cries an enthusiastic new-comer.

It is indeed a glorious evening. Just watch across the Neva the remains of the sunset over Vassali Ostroff! What a marvellous combination of colour in the sky! How deeply calm and lovely are the heavens, from the horizon to the zenith! What exquisite colouring of blues, purples, reds, yellows, greens, and tints of yellow-green, with broad streaks of light, widespread oceans, golden islands, amethyst promontories, unfathomable abysses of glory—all are there, and they will remain there till early dawn, at two o'clock, in unchanged, undecaying beauty, while we bid them good-night, and go sleep!

I confess to the disappointment which I have always experienced when comparing any place I have ever visited with the best descriptions of it which I had previously read.

The pictures drawn by the writers, or perhaps these as misrepresented by the mind of the reader, have never at once adjusted themselves to the actual reality.

A revolution is necessary, in order to exchange the old image of the fancy for the new one of the eye. Mountains, lakes, and rivers, require a new arrangement—yet the descriptions may have been admirable, and, when read on the spot, have probably assisted in pointing out beauties and features of the landscape which otherwise might have escaped our notice. With this experience I will not attempt to describe in detail, but only very generally, what I saw in St. Petersburg and Moscow.

At the beginning of the last century, the site on which the capital is now built was a dreary morass, shaded by the primitive forest, and, like a huge black sponge, was charged with moisture from absorbing, since creation, the waters of the Neva that flowed through it and over it as they pleased.

The Czar Peter, a giant man, with a giant's will, boots, and walking stick, and with a genius which bordered on insanity, determined, as all the world knows, that here should be built the capital of his Empire. And so, after having learned shipbuilding and other useful handicrafts, while he lived in that small wooden house in Holland—which I have visited with all tourists to that wet, flat land of ditches, canals, and windmills—the said Peter built a similar hut among the marshes of "the Islands" of the Neva, and began to drive piles, build quays, and accumulate stones, to rear a new Amsterdam.

Peter determined to have ships, to beat the Swedes, and thus gain the command of the Northern Sea, and open a grand gate to his future empire—how much greater since his day!—and also to have always open a back-door to Europe.

The genial spirit of the great man is well illustrated in his reception of the first ship which entered his new port.

The story is told how a ship was sailing in the northern seas, loaded with cargo for the market of Revel, at that time a notable and flourishing port. The cargo was valuable, and the time to reach the port for the market was short.

"If the wind hold fair," said Auke, the owner and helmsman of the ship, to Karl the merchant-owner of its cargo, "we shall make the port before noon to-day. Yonder is the gulf just coming in sight."

The wind was then doubtful, but soon it rose into a

gale. Long before noon the sea and wind and clouds seemed mingled in a common fury.

Through the storm, Auke heard the sound of a bell. "A bell!" cried he, "there's a ship somewhere in trouble."

He put his ship about in the direction of the sound.

"What are you doing?" said Karl.

"Doing? I am steering for that ship."

"Steer for Revel, Auke, I command you, steer for Revel; we shall miss the market, and I'm a ruined man!"

"Heaven help you, then!" said Auke firmly, "for I am for that ship."

At this moment a small boat was sighted. It was fixed on a bank. Two or three miserable men clung to its rigging, and mountain breakers washed over it.

"Out with the boat," cried Auke, and the sailors looked alarmed.

Karl protested that it was madness. "What! lose the market, and ship, and all!"

"Lose everything, sir, but self-respect," said Auke, fixing his eye so as to bring his ship as near as he dare come to the wreck. "I cannot leave them, sir; I won't! It may be your plight and mine some day. Man the boat!"

The sailors obeyed. Auke left the helm with the mate, and himself took charge of the boat for the rescue.

Surely it was an awful yet grand sight even to Karl, to see the brave man bent on his mission of mercy, in his tiny boat, amid that terrible sea.

One by one the miserable fellows were got from the rigging, and Auke and his prize were safely on board his ship again.

But now the chance of the market was gone. They had missed their tide, got themselves into the teeth of the wind, and were bound to put for shelter into the Neva, a Russian river on which the Czar was then building his new town.

Karl was, therefore, still more angry with his helmsman, and said to him, "The cargo will be robbed, and we shall be made into serfs, and compelled to work on the walls of the town."

"Well, well," said Auke, "we've done our duty, whatever comes. I could not leave that ship."

Karl said no more. The ship was now flying before the storm at a terrific speed, Auke keeping her head to the river's mouth.

Now, one month before this, Peter the Great had laid the first stone of St. Petersburg. There was no town yet, and Peter the Great had not yet earned the name of Great. He was very little known, and the town he was to build was less known.

For the new town, however, these disappointed, storm-driven seamen were unconsciously making as fast as their canvas would carry them. This canvas was no sooner seen at the little town of St. Petersburg than a great stir arose.

"Please your Majesty," said one of the excited courtiers of the Czar, "there is a large ship standing in the Neva."

ST. PETERSBURG. 91

"Ship!" replied the Czar; "the first to my town; it must be honoured. Where is it? Get me out a boat."

The boat was got out, and richly-clad courtiers and officials accompanied the Czar to go on board the new arrival.

Karl saw the approaching boat. "There they come," said he, pale with fear, "as I said. That's you, Auke."

THE CZAR AND KARL.

Auke himself now began to fear, and was half disposed to put his ship round and face, as best he could, the storm.

Second thoughts prevailed, and the brave helmsman awaited, with Karl, his fate.

By this time Peter was at the ship's side. Karl met

him, and implored mercy, and blamed poor Auke. "We've missed our market at Revel," said he, "and have put in only for shelter. Pray let us shelter, your Majesty!"

"No fear, brave fellows. Welcome, welcome to my new port. Your ship is the first bark that ever sailed to my new town. Henceforth she is duty free, whatever she brings for a cargo. Come to my town, and we'll toast to your health."

Karl and Auke landed, the rescued crew landed too.

Karl's cargo was bought at a price which more than satisfied him, and the trade which then began made him one of the wealthiest merchants of Europe, and the town one of its wealthiest ports.

We may in passing add that Auke's words, when full of fear he sailed up the Neva, often came to Karl, "Well, well, we've done our duty, whatever comes;" and no man more frequently in public and in private gave the advice to the young, "Well, well, do your duty, whatever comes."

Peter ordered every strange ship to bring thirty paving stones as a part of her cargo, and every boat ten, and every land carriage three, and the stones accumulated, and the city was built. All his plans succeeded. When he beat Charles XII. at Pultowa in 1709, he exclaimed that "the foundations of St. Petersburg at length stood firm."

He fought many enemies, but the Neva was his greatest, and may yet prove one of the most invincible if provoked by any opposition of the Baltic. Twenty-five feet of rise,

ST. PETERSBURG. 93

such as has occurred, will probably decide the battle against the capital of the Czars. But for more than a century and a half Peter's plans have beat the Neva's stream.

Upwards of 600 streets cover the surface of the morass, 12,000 public and private conveyances drive over it, 11,000 shops and stalls adorn it, and half a million of people live upon it.

But, alas! the morass has so far its triumphs. If a pit is dug in any part of the town, three feet deep, the water oozes from its sides and bottom. This probably affects the health of the population, as the deaths every year exceed the births by 8,000.

Knowing the admiration which most travellers have expressed for St. Petersburg, I am almost afraid to acknowledge my great disappointment with it. It by no means came up to what I expected from the description I had read, or the "illustrations" I had seen of it.

The finest view, I think, is from the centre of the Admiralty, in that grand open space where 100,000 men may be manœuvred. In front is the Nevskoi Prospect, one of the widest streets in Europe, and stretching in a straight line for three miles. To the left is the noble Alexander column, flanked on one side by the Winter and Hermitage Palaces, and on the other by the handsome quadrant of public offices, opening by a large arch into streets beyond, having on its summit a car of victory. The extreme right of the view, and of the place, is bounded by the buildings of the Holy Synods, and the farthest angle filled up by St. Isaac's Cathedral.

The open space on the opposite side to St. Isaac's, and next the Neva, is marked by the statue of the Czar Peter; while beyond the broad, noble river itself appear the long buildings on the quays of the islands. There is no doubt a vastness in the scale of this Place d'Armes which is imposing. There are, moreover, details in this great whole which stand minute examination. St. Isaac's Church—which by the way cost about, as some say, £16,000,000!—is a stately and solid building without, but too bizarre within, and too over-loaded with gildings, and too flash with colour, to produce the solemn effects of York or Westminster as a place of worship. It is, however, admirably adapted for those spectacles in which the Greek Church delights.

The Hermitage Palace, with its noble staircase and magnificent collection of paintings, is worthy in every respect of a great capital; nor is there any monolith in Europe to be compared with the Alexander Column, the shaft alone being eighty feet of unbroken polished granite. But in spite of all this, and much more which might be said in favour of other views and of particular objects, the general impression which the whole made on me irresistibly was that of a rapidly-got-up city, with a singularly waste and unfinished look about it, barbaric vastness and oriental display, without real, endurable, unmistakable grandeur. The platform or base-line from which the buildings spring is ugly, being a desert of uneven stones, full of mud or dust-holes, open waterways, and undulations, excruciating to the miserable travellers in a drosky. This sadly mars the general aspect.

The vast majority of the palaces are mere brick and stucco, with a very decayed, shabby look about them, while the immense space seems to dwarf every building into paltry dimensions, and themselves to appear empty of people, who are but dots on their acres of surface.

The Nevskoi Prospect has nothing very striking in it, except its breadth and length. The shop-windows are small, owing, I presume, to the necessities of winter; the show of goods is commonplace; the pavement, wretched and uncomfortable, made up of round, flinty stones, or uneven blocks of wood; the equipages are mean; the passengers, on the whole, poor looking; while every street seems to end at last in wretched houses, dreary spaces, with horses, carts, and all sorts of rubbish; and, finally, to be lost in "nowhere," unless in the primeval forest or morass.

Then there is the absence of monumental interest. No doubt, to the native of Russia, many "vitches," and "ditches," and "offs," are full of patriotic remembrances. But most travellers, like myself, have never heard of these names, or the deeds which have made them illustrious, performed beyond the Caucasus.

The Czars are, in fact, the nation to a stranger. One knows and hears only of them—the great, the mad, the bad, the murdered, from Peter down to our late enemy Nicholas, who combined not a few of these characteristics.

The associations which chiefly fill the mind are connected with immense armies, distant conquests, Cossacks, the knout, serfs, political criminals, Siberia, with a Czar over all, and a background of bribery, and of political and moral corruption, which darkens the whole Russian sky.

The finest sights in St. Petersburg are the great bazaars and the islands. The former are thoroughly

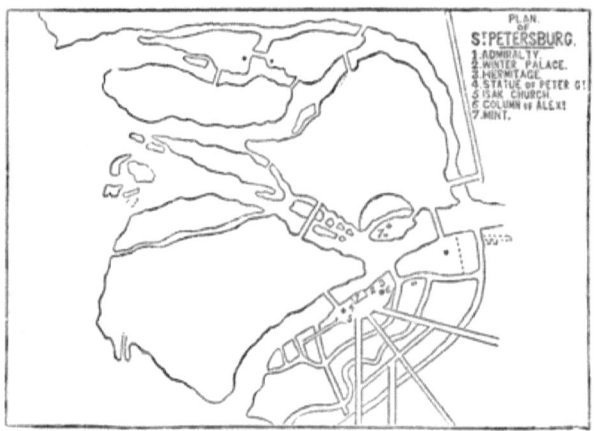

MAP OF ST. PETERSBURG AND THE ISLANDS.

Russian and oriental, and there is no stroll so interesting as through those interminable arcades, perfectly sheltered from the rain, and admitting as much daylight from above as is desirable, with the open warehouses, containing every article bought and sold over a counter in Russia, and swarming with the most motley assemblage of buyers and sellers to be anywhere seen.

ST. PETERSBURG. 97

The drive through the islands was to me peculiarly interesting from its endless extent, the presence of uncultivated, untouched nature, with her Neva streams and quiet Baltic inlets, and primeval trees, and peasant-houses, as rude as if in a distant forest; while everywhere are as unexpectedly met with, the country seats and beautiful cottages of wealthy citizens, and here and there cafés and

PEASANTS' HOUSES.

theatres, and scenes of gay amusement, as false and gaudy as in the Champs-Elysées. On the whole, wild nature has the best of it.

But perhaps the finest feature in St. Petersburg is the noble Neva! The hotels are filthy; the police, villains; the droskies, tortures; the palaces, shams; the natives, ugly; but the Neva seems to redeem all! It flows on, deep, pure, rapid, proud, and majestic; whether one gazes on its waters flowing beneath sun-set, crosses them in the light and painted ferry-boats, quaffs them, or bathes in them, one is in no case disappointed.

But why should we express any astonishment that this great capital should in any respect disappoint us? The wonder rather is that such a city has risen in such a country in so short a time. Old General Wilson told me that he had, when a child, been spoken to by " Catherine the Great," whom he distinctly remembered, and she was married to Peter the Third, the grandson of Peter the First, who founded St. Petersburg.

NORTHERN RUSSIA.

CHAPTER IV.

MOSCOW.

I LONGED to see the real old capital of Russia. Yet I had no preconceived idea of it in my mind, except that of an undefined picture of a mysterious old Kremlin, with flames and smoke surrounding it, and Napoleon beginning his terrible march from the unexpected cold. I was happy, therefore, to find myself in the train, which was snorting along its iron path *en route* to the Kremlin.

I have little to say about the journey. It occupies about eighteen hours, the distance being 400 miles. The line is as straight as an arrow, and quite as uninteresting. It passes through a forest as prosaic as a few brooms stuck in a marsh. No tunnel darkens it; no cutting flanks it. Not a town is seen along its course; for though a few are stations, yet the station-house alone is visible. I would have liked to have stopped at Tver, on one of the branches of the Volga, and the starting point of the steam navigation down that noble river.

The route is extremely comfortable by the railway to Moscow, the carriages, as everywhere else, being far superior to those in Britain, especially the second class. The officials are most civil. The refreshment rooms are equal to any in Europe, and the tea unrivalled.

RUSSIAN TEA-SELLERS.

I cannot mention its name without expressing my thankful acknowledgment for this one unmatched Russian luxury. The Russian tea, or "Tchai," is the product, I have been told, of provinces in China too far north to be able to supply the European markets through the southern ports of the Empire. It is conveyed overland to Russia, packed in skins, which are seen in the tea-shops, in parcels about a yard square. It is consequently more expensive than our tea, its price varying from 8s. to upwards of 20s. the pound. But a much smaller quantity is required to make a cup, or rather a tumbler, as it is only in such that tea is served in Russia. It is the universal and most refreshing beverage, and costs to the drinker, as far as I remember, about 6d. a glass. In some of the "Tractirs" or restaurants of Moscow, such as the famous one near the Exchange, about forty pounds' weight of tea are consumed daily.

The food supplied at the principal railway stations had nothing which I could discover very peculiar about it, except its general excellence. The Russian dishes, *par excellence*, must be demanded by the traveller before they can be obtained.

In the best restaurants of Moscow, where one sees two friends eating with their spoons out of one tureen, he naturally assumes that this is a national rather than an individual custom; and, when dining out, he may probably be startled by his iced soup with cold salmon in it. But along the railway he is not reminded by the cooking of his distance from France or England, except by the high charges for wine above the former, and by the abundance of time granted at every station for meals, as compared with the latter.

Next to tea, the common drink is excellent beer, or "piva," and a sour but not unpleasant acid decoction, void of alcohol, called *quass*.

The supplies of fruit are neither cheap nor tempting. Most of it comes from the south.

The stoppages on the railway are frequent and long. But a walk and saunter refresh the system, and I saw several really nice-looking young ladies, who were in the same carriage with us, employ these seasons of repose to smoke their cigarettes, which they did with such grace as unfortunately to tempt both strangers and foreigners to follow their bad example.

I found myself early in the forenoon in the busy parlour of Mr. Billo, well known to all travellers to Moscow as a most civil landlord.

" To the Kremlin!" was the first and anxious desire of our party. So to the Kremlin we went.

How shall I describe it? for it is unquestionably one of the most remarkable, odd, out-of-the-way, like-nothing-else spots I have ever visited, and indeed *the* thing to be seen in Moscow, if not in Russia.

The first sign of the Kremlin, as we walked along the street towards it, was a high whitewashed wall, with Tartar-like embrasures, and separated from the town by an open boulevard. Beyond this nothing was visible; until, on passing through a gateway, behind which was a very small chapel, which seemed from its lamps, its pictures, and crowded worshippers to be some "holy place," we entered on what seemed a busy town. This was the "Kitai Gorod" or Chinese city.

Proceeding along the narrow crowded street, we debouched into a vast oblong space, half a mile or so in length, and about half this or less in breadth. This was the *krasnoi ploschad* (red place).

The one side was bounded, opposite to us, and also to the right, by another high whitewashed wall, with towers, which contained the Kremlin proper; the other side by

THE CATHEDRAL OF ST. BASIL.

the back of the low houses of the great bazaar. The end to the left was occupied by that most fantastical and indescribable of all buildings, that compound of twenty domes of different shapes and sizes, of stairs, and chapels, and mass of colour, blue, green, yellow, white, red, and gilt; that Tartar-like Chinese Pagoda (ridiculous were it not so venerated), and the venerable Basil, the Cathedral of St. Basil or Basiliki Blagennoi.

Nearly opposite this church is the sacred entrance to the Kremlin, by the Holy Gate or the "Spass vorota." Over it there hangs, under a glass, and before a lamp which burns from age to age, a picture of the Saviour. From various traditions, which need not here be enumerated, every passenger, high and low, from the Emperor to the serf, must keep off his hat as he passes through this covered archway, which leads upwards, by a slight ascent of a few yards, to the acropolis and capital of Moscow. So have passed many a stately procession, many a weary pilgrim, many a conqueror and soldier from conquests extending from Paris to Persia, and from the Volga to the Amoor.

Bareheaded, I found myself at last on the stone plateau of the old Kremlin. Anxious to get a bird's-eye view of the whole before examining any of its details, I directed my steps at once to the highest point in the city, the summit of the high tower of "Ivan Valiki," or Long John.

But I could not help pausing as I recalled an early dream which, along with many others, was suggested by a dear old book I have long since lost sight of, called *Ten Wonders of the World*, a dream now realised in the "Great Bell of Moscow." There it lay, the "Tzar Kolokoi," or King of Bells, a huge inverted cup, twenty-one feet high, and upwards of sixty feet in circumference, whose very metal is worth £350,000, and with a piece out of its side which leaves a door open for easy access to the curious who wish to visit its ample interior. What a tongueless mouth! What a dead thunderer! But we must ascend the tower. We first pass a huge bell

THE GREAT BELL OF MOSCOW.

which in size looks like the eldest son or wife of the dead one below, weighing about sixty-four tons, and requiring three men to swing its clapper; then up another storey, meeting about fifty more bells, diminishing in size as the summit of the tower is reached—yet the least of them great.

When the summit is at last attained, let a cursory glance only be given at the Kremlin below, and at Moscow beyond, through the clear, transparent, and brilliant atmosphere, and then, perhaps, for the first time, one feels amply repaid for coming so far to gaze on such a peculiar and wonderful spectacle.

Immediately below is the flat summit of the low hill which is properly called the Kremlin or fortress, and which occupies about a mile square. Rising out of this flat plateau, and without apparent order, but closely grouped together, are about sixty gilded domes, marking the oldest and most revered churches in Russia—with palaces for metropolitans, bishops, and czars, old as the Tartars, and modern as Nicholas; with treasuries, arsenals, and nunneries. And then there are the walls of all the buildings whitewashed with snowy whiteness, topped with coloured roofs of every hue; the vacant spots and small squares dividing the closely-packed buildings, occupied by thronging worshippers, soldiers, monks, nuns, and pilgrims, all clearly defined in their many shadows in the pure atmosphere; while the visible portion of the wall, which bounds the view on two sides, is so singularly picturesque in old, curious watch-towers, mouldering turrets, all covered with coloured tiles—all making up a most remarkable picture. But when the eye passed from the more immediate objects beneath, and took in the rude panorama beyond, the spectacle was magnificent.

MOSCOW.

On one side, the river Moskwa curled itself like a snake, one of its bends being immediately under the Kremlin walls. Farther away, a few miles to the right, rose a low ridge of hills or steep wooded banks, called the Sparrow Hills, whose base was washed by the river, from which the whole city first burst upon the gaze of Napoleon and his army; and after visiting the scene, I can hardly imagine a more imposing view of a vast city.

In turning to the other side, to gaze on the city from the summit of the tower, what can be finer? It covers a great area for its population (which is only about 500,000), chiefly owing to the fact of most of the houses standing apart, and having gardens attached to them.

The characteristic feature unquestionably of the city is its churches. How many there are of those I know not (it is said 600), for I tried in vain to count them. But as each has several copper-covered, gilded, or ornamental domes (generally five), with high gilded crosses, and these everywhere glittering in the sun, mingling with the green of the trees and the white of their houses, all form a most brilliant and singular panorama, spread over a great area. Add to this the domes of great monasteries, such as the Seminoff and Donskoi (sacred to the Don Cossacks), which gleam to right and left beyond the city, on the banks of the Moskwa, and the brilliant impression which the gazer receives from the summit of Ivan Valiki is deepened.

It is a spectacle which one never tires of, and few travellers grudge the toil of a second ascent, at least, in even the hottest weather, to have the splendid vision renewed.

Before leaving this "standpoint," the mystery of the walls within walls around the Kremlin is explained. These but represent the defences built at different times as the town extended beyond the "fortress," which occupied the summit of the highest point, for hill it can hardly be called, in the original Muscovite settlement of the fourteenth century.

Perhaps the reader asks, whether "the great fire" of 1812, which roasted the French out of the capital into the frost, has not altered the features of the city?

I could see no evidences of the fire, nor were any changes in the town pointed out between what it was and is, which enabled me in the least degree to realise its effects. The Kremlin was saved. But the line of retreat which Napoleon himself was obliged to follow, in order to pass with his staff from the Kremlin to the Palace of Petrovski, in the northern suburbs, and from whence he gazed on the tremendous conflagration, is easily traced, and from its detour, indicates a great area of fire, which barred his progress by the more direct route. Nor has it in reality been ascertained with any certainty how the fire originated.

Many of the romantic stories told about it have been denied. The Emperor Alexander repeatedly declared that he had never sanctioned it; and the then Governor of Moscow, Rostopchin, who was thought to have first set his own palace on fire, published a pamphlet, asserting that the whole thing was accidental! Whatever glory, therefore, has been attributed to **the Russians,** for this supposed grand sacrifice, **has been thrust upon them** by others, but rejected by themselves.

But we must **descend from** Long John and examine the Kremlin, its **churches,** nunneries, palaces, treasury.

Impossible! The mere catalogue of its curiosities **would** occupy **pages.** We should be compelled to degenerate into the "Look **now before you, and here you** see," &c., of the penny showman. Yet, without doubt, a collection of objects are here congregated expressive **of** the history and rise of Russia.

The palaces **are** extremely **interesting. The New** Palace has the most magnificent **suite of** apartments **I** have ever seen. **The St. George's,** Alexander's, St. Andrew's, St. **Catherine's, in** which the knights of those several orders are invested, **are** finer than any **in** St. Petersburg, and **are not** surpassed by any **in the** world. The **old** Tartar palace, with its low-roofed small apart**ments,** almost closets, its narrow screw staircase **to the** council-chamber, its thrones, **beds,** arabesque **and fantas**tic ornaments on the walls of trees with birds, and fruits, squirrels, mice, painted in every colour, are all thoroughly Oriental and Moorish. It was from the roof of this palace that Napoleon first beheld Moscow, **from within** the walls; and the view is **superb.**

The treasury, again, is **a** world in itself **of** national curiosities. **It contains, among** other provincial **wonders, the** crowns of all her emperors, and those of the several countries they have conquered, including the crown and sceptre (broken, too!) of Poland; crowns dating as far back as the twelfth century, and all sparkling with clusters of jewels of immense value and splendour. The thrones, too, are there—one of massive silver, all enriched with jewels—on which successive czars have sat, most of them uncomfortably, I doubt not; and huge gilded chariots, like those in old pictures of Lord Mayor's shows, with wheels and harness suited to a menagerie, in which these bears of the north have driven; and the clothes, which these same czars have worn on State occasions; with things innumerable, including Napoleon's camp-bed, and the chair which Charles XII. used at the battle of Pultowa.

In passing out of this treasury, 900 cannon taken in war are seen arranged in the Place d'Armes. The most of them were taken from the French, in their retreat, by their victorious but barbarous pursuers. I need hardly say, that no specimens of English cannon are there. These are guns too rare to be found in foreign arsenals. "Our national vanity is great!" laments the foreigner. It may be so, but I trust our national gratitude is greater. Wellington never lost a gun.

But I am forgetting the Kremlin. What else have we to see there? Why, the *valet de place* tells us we "have seen nothing;" and that, too, after pacing for hours, under oppressive heat—" up-stairs, down-stairs, and in my lady's chamber."

We have yet to see, he says, the Palace of the Patriarch, with its venerable public halls; and the House of the Holy Synod, with its ancient library; and its halls with the two great silver kettles, and thirty silver jars, in which the holy oil, or "*mir*," is manufactured, having as its *elixir vitæ* drops of the oil from the flask used by Mary Magdalene when she anointed Christ's feet. This is sent to every part of the empire, to anoint infants when baptized, from the "vitches" of the Czar down to queer-looking creatures beyond the Caspian, among the forests of Siberia, near the walls of China, or on the shores of the Arctic Ocean; and applied also to the dying, who are passing into the land where there is neither barbarian, Scythian, bond, nor free.

We have also to enter the Cathedral of the Archangel Michael, so holy to the Russians. Just glance at that fresco of Jonah, in which there are three Jonahs, each with his name over his head; one Jonah thrown overboard, the other disgorged, and the other received by the King of Nineveh. What a delightful and primitive combination of ship, waves, whale, sailors, prophet or prophets, kings, and nobles, with Nineveh itself, in that space above the door! Within are the tombs, side by side, like huge coffins, of the Russian monarchs down to Peter the Great.

There is also the Church of the Annunciation, in which the czars are crowned, paved with jasper, agate, and cornelian (without beauty), having the throne of the czars, and relics without number, gold and silver counted by the pound weight, and with a picture of the Virgin

Mother, painted by St. Luke—the only real and authentic one, of course; and with a real drop of blood, no doubt, which once belonged to John the Baptist.

And after that we shall visit the great Military School, capable of drilling within its four walls, and beneath one roof, eight thousand men; and the Foundling Hospital, and—and—

In some such strain as this, our well-informed, intelligent bore, the *valet de place*, addressed us on the Kremlin, when the sun was pouring down its hottest rays, and these were reflected from the stone pavement, which glowed like a furnace.

I have too intense a memory of the utter hopelessness of " doing " these wonders, and many more, satisfactorily to repeat the dose, even in fancy, to my readers. They are, I doubt not, almost as tired by this recital of the sights as I was by the reality. I resolved to take a Russian bath.

" What like was it ? "

Pardon me if I do not reveal the mystery, beyond stating that it was very hot, very soapy, very dear, very barbarous, and utterly indescribable.

NORTHERN RUSSIA.

CHAPTER V.

MANNERS AND CUSTOMS.

AN ordinary amount of common sense, apart from an ordinary amount of experience from travel in foreign countries, may suffice to teach a man the absurdity of giving forth his opinions, with the slightest confidence in their being founded on sufficient evidence, regarding the political or social condition, from his own observation, of any country which he has visited for a few weeks only.

The first day I landed in the United States, I took my seat on the top of an omnibus—by no means an aristocratic position, but a most interesting one in passing through the streets of a great city—when my attention was called to the fact of the driver seating himself on the *left* or "off" side of the ample "Box."

With the disposition of a traveller to watch for national characteristics, I was inclined to "book" this fact as peculiar to drivers in America. But I thought it best, before doing so, to inquire into the cause of this unusual phenomenon.

"Pray, why do you sit on that side?" I inquired.

"'Cause, stranger, I guess I'm left-handed!"

I gained some experience by this reply, and resolved, accordingly, never to generalize too hastily, lest I should make mere exceptions prove the rule of manners and customs.

I don't wish to forget this principle in presuming to speak about the Russians. But, just as a Parliamentary committee, which itself knows little of a subject, nevertheless obtains information by examining competent witnesses, so may a traveller have opportunities abroad of examining those who *ought* to possess information from long residence, and whose evidence he has the means of constantly sifting, and in some degree of testing, by his own limited observation. Accordingly, I naturally embraced every opportunity given me of ascertaining what those long resident in Russia knew about its people. Circumstances enabled me to come into contact with several well-informed persons, whose character for truth was above suspicion.

Well, then, let me give my readers a specimen of one conversation of several I had with such witnesses. I do not pretend to give the very words, nor the exact sequence of the remarks.

The dinner is ended; the clatter of plates and of all the European languages has ceased; the most of the guests have dispersed—some have gone out on pleasure or business, some to read the newspapers in the next room, and others to arrange about their journey to the great fair, then going on at Nijni Novogorod. But at the end of the empty table, half a dozen Englishmen and Scotchmen have remained, by special invitation, to chat with the travellers who have brought some of them letters of introduction.

One man has been twenty years at the head of prosperous works for the manufacture of machinery; another, nine years in a similar business; another, fifteen years a superintendent of one of the largest cotton mills; two others, partners in an establishment which has necessitated a large amount of travelling for sixteen years in every part of Russia; while one or two more are acquainted with the country during a residence of several years, either in Moscow or in St. Petersburg.

Such are the witnesses. Let us examine them on several points.

We begin.

"One hears a great deal about the Russian police," was remarked, "but it is difficult to know how far the stories recorded of them in anonymous books are true, or how far they may be the mere invectives or inventions of men who suffered righteously from them."

"A greater set of scoundrels don't exist!" pronounces

my cotton friend, calmly and coolly, as if speaking from the heart.

"Ha! ha! ha! my boy, you are sore upon the point," said an acquaintance of his, sitting beside him.

"Now do tell our friends about what happened to yourself the other day. It is a fair specimen of the set," suggests a third party.

After some joking and coaxing, the story was told. But I wish my readers could have seen the figure of the splendid Yorkshireman who told it. He was upwards of six feet, with a bronzed, handsome face, and light curly hair, and fists from whose grasp most men would shrink if they seized in order to shake! I wish also, if the reader loves Yorkshire as I do, that he heard the story told in the dialect of the great county, so full of force and humour.

The story ran thus:—The cotton mills had suffered, more than once, considerable losses in their cotton bales. It was difficult to detect the thief—for no doubt the bales were stolen—and difficult, when he was detected, to convict him. So utterly corrupt is justice, from the highest to the lowest, so combined are all interested parties to act solely with reference to their own probable gain in money, that it is always a very complex problem to solve, whether more is lost or gained by ever going into court in order to recover property. The bribery is so immense, so shameful, and reduced to such a science and art, that the complainer is always in the dark; for the police he employs to search, the advocate he employs to plead, the judge who tries the case—each and all may be bribed by higher sums on the part of the defender than on that of the complainer. Therefore, in Russia alone can the rule be followed by selfishness, of permitting him who takes your coat to take your cloak also, rather than go to law. But in this case a carrier volunteered (for a *consideration*) certain intelligence regarding the missing cotton bags.

A RUSSIAN SUMMER CARRIAGE.

It was thus discovered that the son of one of the leading merchants in Moscow, and a member of its highest "guild," had been in the habit of bribing the carriers of the cotton to drop a bag occasionally at a certain spot in a wood near the public road, and from which the "gentleman" picked it up shortly afterwards.

Mr. S. laid his scheme of detection founded on this

information. He armed himself with a loaded revolver, and hid himself in the wood, in the environs of Moscow, to watch his prey. The carrier appeared in due time; dropped and concealed the cotton bale in the wood; passed on; and in a short time was followed by the young merchant in his drosky, accompanied by an empty cart. The bale was conveyed into the empty cart by its driver, and, along with the drosky and *its* driver, was proceeding on their journey, when the Moscow gentleman found himself suddenly seized by a huge man who sprang into his vehicle beside him, threatening to shoot him if he offered any opposition while pinioning his hands. A mouse might as well have opposed a wild cat! Mr. S. drove him to the police-office of the district.

Now it so happened that the head police-officer was bribed by Mr. S.

"Bribed!" I exclaimed, interrupting his story; "how could *you* do that?" A general smile prevailed on the countenances of the company, while Mr. S. replied—

"Every man *must* bribe in this country. It is a tax, understood and fixed. Unless merchants bribed the post-office——"

"At what rate?"

"I know some houses that pay about £1 a week; and the merchant who refused this would not get his letters until long after they were due. Unless we bribed the police, neither we nor they could live. For example, the police-officer I speak of only receives as his nominal salary say £100. But he has to keep four horses and two assistants, each at £50 per annum, while his allowance for his horse goes as *his* bribe to his superintendent. How then **is he to** live, unless we pay him? **We** give him about **£20 a** year, and this is absolutely necessary **to secure that his** services shall not be *against* us."

To continue the story. **Mr. S.** appeared with his **prisoner at the bureau of the police-office,** and found **himself** immediately charged **by him** with an attempt at murder, while he denied, at **the same time,** all knowledge of the transaction regarding the cotton, which he was ready to swear he had **never seen or touched!**

The tables **thus seemed** suddenly **turned** against **the** Yorkshireman. But while he, **the young** gentleman, was drawing **up his** protest **and** charge, the police-officer gave a **sign to** Mr. S. to **follow** him to the next room.

"Pray, **Mr. S.,** *was* your pistol loaded?"

"**It** was, and no mistake!"

"**Then** draw the bullet instantly, **or** you will find **yourself** in a scrape."

Mr. **S.** tried to do so in vain, but the policeman effectually aided him. They **returned** to **the room,** and the charge was presented.

"**I see,**" said the officer, "**that you** charge this highly respectable foreigner **with a** threat to shoot you! Pooh! pooh! It was all **a joke!**"

"**Joke!** I wish you had only seen him! Joke!"

"**But** are you sure there were bullets in his **pistol? Mr. S.,** please inform me as to this fact."

Mr. S. instantly handed the pistol to the policeman, and asked him to examine and decide for himself.

"I knew it! The barrels are empty! I cannot tolerate this stupid charge; it is malicious and shameful! Please compromise matters. I presume, Mr. S., *you* are willing to admit that there is no *proof* that this gentleman stole your cotton? and *you*, sir," addressing the Russian, "must admit that there is no proof that Mr. S. intended to do anything else but to give you a fright."

And so a compromise in these terms was agreed upon. But the policeman whispered to Mr. S.—

"Would you like to thrash the rascal? for, if so, I can easily give you an opportunity of doing so, eh?"

But Mr. S. declined the honour. "For," said he, as he told the story, "I knew that the policeman was another rascal, and that, if I had accepted the privilege offered to me, he would have kept it over my head for years, and threatened me with a trial; and every time I attempted to leave the country the trial would be reopened anew, until they were heavily bribed to let me off without it!"

So both parties left the office. But, as the door was closed behind them, the young Russian merchant, finding himself alone with Mr. S., put his finger to his nose and said—

"When you wish to catch a thief again, pray let me advise you to take a little more time, to restrain your passion, to be more careful of evidence, and you may probably succeed; in the meantime, *I rather think I have done you!*" And with a triumphant laugh and bow, he bade Mr. S. a good afternoon.

This fact, which had happened a few weeks before, is a fair specimen of the stories which were told illustrative of the police, and is characteristic of the whole system of "justice" from the highest to the lowest. There is nothing, in fact, in the civilized world more infamous than the execution of the civil and criminal law in Russia.

One other trifling incident I cannot help recording.

"Well, S.," asked one of the company, "how do you and the government doctor get on now?"

"Better a little," replied S. "Do you know, I have found out the reason why the fellow annoyed us so much, and made so many complaints. I know he was a drunkard, and that he insisted on being supplied well with liquor as *his* bribe. So, as I did not drink myself, I hired a man, and paid him regular wages, to drink with the medical inspector. Was that not liberal? But the rascal got offended, and determined to revenge himself on me, because I drank with him by proxy, and did not give him my own company!"

"Are you afraid," I asked another person present, "to travel on the roads at night?"

"Never, unless we meet the Cossack mounted police, who are sure to rob if they catch an unarmed traveller!"

So much for the police. But this led to a further conversation on the cotton mills, working classes, and general morality.

There are in Russia about 140 cotton mills, containing

1,600,000 spindles. Taking all things into account, the protection of the trade raises the price of the article fifty per cent. above England. Smuggling, therefore, exists to a great extent. The workmen employed are serfs,* who generally live in the country, but leave their villages and their wives behind them to work for a time at the factories. Their wages amount to about £2 10s. monthly. Barracks are provided for the workmen. The work is continued by relays day and night. Out of 280 workdays, about 30 are fast or feast days, in which no work is done.

The Russians have hitherto been unable to make good factory machinery; any who have succeeded, apparently, in doing so, have really been indebted to England for its chief portions.

The habits and morals of the working classes are of the lowest possible description. It would be impossible to publish in these pages the unquestionable facts illustrative of their depraved condition. Virtue and truth seem scarcely known. As regards stealing, not one working man or woman is ever permitted to pass out of the premises without being carefully searched by persons employed for this purpose. In spite of this, they manage to pilfer cotton and other articles. Baths are regularly taken weekly, but during the other days their persons are filthy. They lie on bare boards, and never

---

* This was written before 1863, in which year the serfs were emancipated; but the improvement of their intellectual and moral condition will be a work of time.

change their clothes. When a new and commodious lodging-house was built for the workmen of a well-conducted factory at Alexandrofski, near St. Petersburg, the workmen, after examining it, sent a deputation to the manager, who was my informant, asking him what

WORKMEN AT DINNER.

additional wages he meant to give if they went to his new house!

But I have been given to understand that the habits of even the middle and higher classes of society in Moscow and St. Petersburg, with some exceptions, are said to be as polluted as those of the serfs. The moral leprosy is covered with silk garments, and splendid uniforms, and highly respectable outsides, but there it is, nevertheless, in all its vileness. I have never in Austria or France heard, from those best informed as to the state of national morality, of more corruption than exists in Russia. But it is impossible to enter into details on this topic.

Few things gave me a more painful impression of the morality of the people than the Asylum in Moscow—and there is one as great in St. Petersburg—for poor children. The building is magnificent, the education given in it excellent, and all its arrangements princely. Any child brought to it is at once received. I witnessed the process. Two women of the working classes brought each a child. The clerk handed a ticket, with a number attached to it, to be tied round its wrist; a corresponding number was inscribed in the ledger. No questions were asked.

The women delivered up their children with more indifference than most people would part with a cat or dog. The children are next day baptized and vaccinated, and though they may be afterwards claimed, yet the vast majority never are. About sixty children are each day thus received at this one institution. There were in the house about 800 infants, under the care of several hundred nurses. The whole number of children under the charge of the institution is 30,000! The vast majority are boarded out in the country districts.

God preserve to us our family life! And defend us from such premiums upon selfishness and immorality! The poor-laws are bad enough, but this is worse.

But I am forgetting the group at the end of the table. A word or two more, ere we part.

The authentic anecdotes related of the late Emperor during the Crimean war make it more than likely that his mind was latterly affected.

His fits of ungovernable passion, even with old Nesselrode, were notorious. The victory on the Alma, which Nicholas at first would not believe, abusing the officer who brought him the despatch, was known by him for some days before it was made public. An American gentleman, who saw him almost daily among his troops, told me that so changed had he become during that short period, that, without knowing the cause, he had remarked to several friends that the Emperor must be severely ill, and that he looked like a dying man.

The effect of his death was as if some great weight had been taken off society. All acknowledged his power, and felt the presence of a giant among them. But there was an intolerable sense of bondage experienced by all. Liberty of speech was impossible. But since the accession of the present Emperor, men can breathe and speak without fear of a secret police, of secret agents, or of a journey to Siberia. The liberty of the press is every day becoming more unshackled. The police laws, also, which affected the admission, residence, and departure of strangers, are being almost entirely done away with, and brought into harmony with the usages of other European countries. Let us not forget at what a late period of history Russia has entered the European family of nations.

The immense boundaries of Russia extend almost with an unbroken stretch over a hundred degrees of longitude, from the Baltic to the Rocky Mountains, and embrace more than the half of the northern portion of the habitable globe. They descend from the snows of the Arctic Ocean to the burning steppes of Asia. She reigns supreme over a vast and busy population, as well as over hordes of roving barbarians.

Her means of internal communication by her numerous and gigantic rivers; the facilities afforded by her plains and forests for railways and telegraphs; her immense mineral riches and boundless plains of fertile soil; her unassailable military position when on the defensive; her almost unlimited command of men to supply her armies; the subtlety, perseverance, and governing power of her officials; and the hardihood of her people—all promise a future for Russia which, without affording any great cause of alarm to Europe, affords great cause of joyful anticipation to herself, and to all who wish civilisation to supplant barbarianism.

And if to this is added the hope of Christian truth imbuing a Church whose authority is acknowledged by eighty millions of the human race, we may well look with profound interest on all that is taking place in Russia, and from our hearts wish her God-speed in the course on which she has entered.

GREENLAND.

GREENLAND.

CHAPTER I.

THE COAST.

THE coast of Greenland is visited by the whaling ships which annually make their voyages to the icy seas of Davis' Strait and Baffin's Bay; lately by the different exploring vessels sent by the English and American governments to search for Sir John Franklin and his missing companions; and by the Danish ships which, during the navigable season, are dispatched to supply the settlements scattered along the coast with a renewed stock of provisions, and to carry back to Denmark the products of Eskimo hunting and fishing.

Greenland belongs to Denmark, and its trade is monopolized by the government, the Royal Danish Company yearly sending out ships freighted with European goods and provisions, and bringing back skins of the reindeer, seal, walrus, bear, &c., vast quantities of codfish, and occasionally dried salmon.

The Danish settlements and habitations of the Eskimo are situated along the coast from Cape Farewell, the most southern point of Greenland, to lat. 73° N., and at each settlement a governor or chief factor resides with his small staff of Danish officials and workmen. Round them gather a mixed Eskimo population, subsisting by the chase, the results of which they bring to the Danish storehouse, and barter for goods and provisions.

It was in the middle of July that I first saw the coast of Greenland. The mountains in the neighbourhood of Cape Farewell looked in the distance like the teeth of a jagged saw, peak after peak looming out of the mist, and showing their uneven tops covered with snow, which clothed their slopes down to the sea, or inland to the valleys lying between them and the mountains of the interior. No name seemed to be more inappropriate than Greenland; nothing appeared but dark rock and unsullied snow. On landing, however, I found some little vegetation. Greener than other Arctic lands it may be, but to one whose recollections were fresh of the pleasant grassy fields of our own country the name seemed a mockery.

On a nearer approach to the coast, the low land appears stretching out as islands with interlying passages and sounds, barren and bare enough in appearance, but free from snow during the summer. Nearer still, at the distance of a mile or so, there appears a considerable quantity of verdure among the small valleys, though the vegetation which covers them is of a brownish colour. Following the windings which are visible between the islands, we pass up the deeper fiords, where is the greatest quantity of vegetation to be seen in all Greenland: some six or eight miles up the fiords the land is even covered with stunted willow and birch bushes; these are the only representatives of "forests" in this barren land, and never attain a greater height than four feet. The hollows and slopes of the mountains are covered with loose stones of considerable size, barely hidden by these bushes.

The vast icebergs which thickly strew these seas have their origin from the ice-fiords and the coast glaciers, thus: this frozen mass being constantly pushed forward, a sort of outward draught takes place, its surface becomes crevassed and fissured by passing over uneven ground, and the exposed face of the glacier being eaten away by the warm water at its base, becomes top-heavy, breaks away from the mass, and a new child of the Arctic is launched into the world.

The icebergs vary in size according to the glaciers from which they have been formed and the conditions under which they have been separated.

Imagine St. Paul's Cathedral, St. George's Hall, or Holyrood Palace floating upon the surface of the water, having five or six times its own size underneath: picture it made of the purest white marble, carved into innumerable domes, turrets, and spires. Again, imagine some vast island undulated, caverned, and massive, or some immense but mastless *Great Eastern*, glistening in the sun, reflecting hues of the emerald, beryl, and turquoise; here you may see one towering heavenward—

> "As a stately Attic temple
> Rears its white shafts on high;"

then another without a single elevation, presenting to the eye nothing but an irregular crevassed surface.

The spired bergs are not more beautiful than dangerous; the ice navigator knows that they may turn over at any moment; the water in which they float gradually melting that portion which is submerged, the centre of gravity slowly moves up toward the water-line, and the slightest shock is sufficient to upset the whole mass.

The solid, squarish bergs are those used by the shipmasters as temporary moorings. Drawing perhaps some 800 to 1,000 feet they ground and act as anchors to the ships. On these bergs are usually found small lakes of *fresh* water, the ice being of *land* origin. The constant action of the powerful Arctic sun thawing the surface, the water either collects in pools or miniature lakes, or trickles down the side.

It is almost impossible for those who have not seen them to imagine the sublimity and grandeur of a belt of these ice-islands. Their fantastic shapes traced out in pure glistening white against a pale blue sky, floating in water of a still deeper hue, form a picture which but few artists could paint. They strew the Arctic seas in thousands, and float south to be dissolved in the warm waters of the Atlantic, becoming the dread of the navigator of the Newfoundland banks.

The reader may try to conceive the difficulties and dangers which beset vessels navigating the northern seas, and picture the imminence of the peril should they encounter a heavy gale. The air thick with fog and snow-flakes, the ropes stiff with frozen spray, the bitter temperature benumbing the hands and feet, the ship surrounded by huge mountains of ice, roaring and crashing, heaving and rearing, one against the other, and against the poor ship; now she is tossed against the ice, now the ice-blocks beat and bump against her side, masts and yards crack, bells ring, men shout, the storm howls, every minute seems to be the last—

"And the boldest hold their breath for a time."

As we approached the Spitzbergen ice-stream, we found the sea strewed with detached pieces of ice, with occasional small packs some four or five miles in extent, their colour varying from the purest white to a deep blue, according to the shape and the reflected light. The waves surging against the masses sounded like the dashing of the sea against a rocky coast. The wind falling calm, we were enveloped in fog, and had to get up steam to urge our way through this frozen barrier, which often fouled the ship, and caused her to shake from stem to stern, and at times altogether arrested her progress.

The most fantastic shapes were at times assumed by

the ice. I remember one group in particular, the grotesqueness of which was remarkable. It consisted of a gracefully-formed pelican of ice, escorted by a huge water-jug, and both apparently surrounded by barn-door fowls. All round these were multitudes of the most queerly-shaped monsters: you can hardly mention one family of animals which did not seem to have its icy representative,

THE SPITZBERGEN ICE-STREAM.

the oddity of their forms causing as much amusement as the beauty of their tints occasioned admiration.

Having passed through this ice-stream, we still continued our landward course. Finding, however, by the afternoon of the 18th July, that we could not get sight of the shore, we shortened sail, let down steam, and lay-to till the fog should clear off and show us our position.

This it did at six P.M., revealing a beautiful coast-line as it lifted off the land, the landscape bounded by the far inland white mountain-tops, clear cut against the deep blue sky. Farther north, along the coast, we saw the "blink" of the glacier, which there stretches along, or rather forms the coast-line, for eight or ten miles, relieving, with its gleaming whiteness, the sombre aspect of the black and barren peaks of primary rock on either side.

And now we saw a couple of kajaks coming off towards the ship. These kajaks are from eighteen to twenty feet long, tapering to a point at both ends like a weaver's shuttle, some fifteen inches wide, and eight or nine deep, flattish above and convex below. The frame is made of laths of wood, and covered over with sealskin prepared by the Eskimo, and sewed on whilst wet. A small hole is left in the middle, surrounded by a ledge; into this the native "wriggles," sitting with his body at right angles to his legs; then fastening his sealskin shirt, or "jumper," he forms a continuous water-tight surface up to his throat.

Seated thus, with his "payortit," or paddle, held by the middle in his hands, by alternate strokes with its right and left blades he propels the canoe at the rate of six to eight miles per hour, passing through waves and encountering seas which, in an ordinary boat, would be neither safe nor pleasant.

These natives brought us some eider-duck eggs, and received biscuit in exchange. We then stood in toward Frederikshaab, eight or nine bergs appearing in sight, but none very close to us.

GREENLAND.

CHAPTER II.

FREDERIKSHAAB.

THE evening was beautiful, and seemed warm and agreeable compared with the previous one. Cautiously sailing between the islands, guided by an Eskimo pilot, we reached our destination in the morning, and moored near the Danish brig which had arrived with provisions, &c., for the use of the settlement. We were at anchor in a small cove, flanked on either side by hills 600 or 800 feet high. The end of the bay opened to the interior, which, some two or three miles off, was shut in by mountains.

Scarcely was our anchor down before the ship was surrounded by kajaks. Soon numbers of women, girls, and children trooped along the rocks abreast of the ship to the nearest point, where they sat laughing and jabbering to their hearts' content.

On the ladies of the community being pointed out to me, I was rather incredulous; a glance at the portraits

A YOUNG MAN.　　AN OLD WOMAN.　　A YOUNG WOMAN.
(IN SUMMER DRESS.)

will show the reason. The only mark which distinguishes their dress from that of their lords is the presence of a "top-knot." Their hair, instead of being dressed in the ordinary way, is drawn upwards to the crown of the head, and then tied in a knot; this is surrounded by a ribbon, the colour of which varies with the social position of the wearer. Some of them displayed considerable taste in the selection of the pattern of the ribbons, which are, of course, imported from Denmark, and are very probably of English manufacture.

We were speedily visited by the Danish officials, namely, the chief factor, his assistant, and the priest. Dr. Rink, the Royal Inspector of South Greenland, who happened to be at the settlement at the time, also came on board. We found these gentlemen very agreeable and intelligent. The inspector, a man of high scientific acquirements, was promoted to his present position after having been for many years engaged in a mineralogical survey of Greenland. Pastor Barnsfeldt, who, with his wife, had been for some time resident in the country, gave us some interesting statistics, illustrating the social condition of the Eskimos. The assistant-factor had only been two or three years in Greenland. He had formed one of the noble band of volunteers engaged in the war with Sleswig and Holstein; he was a knight of the order of Dannebrog, and wore his decoration. Chief-trader Möller, father-in-law to the inspector, for many years resident in the country, was becoming tired of its monotony, and anxious to return to Copenhagen.

Accompanied by these gentlemen, we went on shore, and partook of their hospitality.

The houses of the officials are all built of wood, thickly

coated on the outside with black tar, the windows and doors being double, and painted white. They are kept spotlessly clean, according to the custom of the Scandinavian peoples. The beams supporting the ceiling are plainly seen, giving to the room an aspect not unlike the ward-room of a man-of-war. The side-panels are painted blue or green, the rest of the walls being white. The stove in the corner is brightly polished; the floor without carpet, and beautifully clean; the windows adorned with a few European garden flowers, which bloom with difficulty in this inhospitable region.

After luncheon, we walked some way into the interior, visiting, on our way, some of the huts. These are essentially dirty and disagreeable to one unused to their ways. The better class have a wooden frame and a window; but the greater part have only a shell made of sods and earth, with a few props of wood or bones of the whale in the inside. The approach to the interior is through a narrow passage some three feet and a half high, opening into the hut, which rises to an elevation of five feet or so. A raised dais serves the purpose of a seat by day and a bedstead by night. On this dais the ladies sit, tailor-fashion, and occupy themselves in domestic work. Cooking is performed by means of a stone lamp hanging at one extremity of the platform, and supplied with blubber and moss.

In a small hut of about six feet square, seven, eight, or even a larger number of persons will contrive to exist; and as personal cleanliness is not a virtue practised by the Eskimos, the heat and the offensive smell may more easily be imagined than described. The ablutions of the men generally consist in moistening their fingers with saliva, and rubbing the salt spray from their faces; the mothers use their tongues, like cats, to clean and polish their children.

The men do not dress their hair in any particular fashion, merely shortening it over the forehead, and allowing it to hang down on the cheeks and neck; the women often wrap a handkerchief round their heads to keep them warm, as the drawing up of the hair to the crown leaves the greater part of the head uncovered.

The shape of the Eskimo face is somewhat oval, the greatest breadth being below the eye, at the cheek bones; the forehead arches upward, ending narrowly; the chin is a blunt cone; the nose is more or less depressed, broad at the base, with somewhat thickened nostrils; the lips thickish, but the teeth generally very white and regular.

Occasionally, among the young women, we saw a good-natured, pretty face; but the old women are frightfully ugly. Their teeth drop out; they discontinue the use of the head-band, showing a bald place where the hair has fallen out by being pulled against the grain; the face, deeply furrowed, assumes a very harsh expression; and the legs are bowed by the constant use of the "tailor posture" while sitting. The resemblance between the sexes is further increased by the absence of beard and moustache among the men, any stray evidence of either being ruthlessly pulled out by means of a couple of shells.

We were not sorry to escape from the stifling atmosphere of the huts; and presently leaving the settlement behind us, and crossing a swampy valley traversed by numerous streams, we proceeded up the mountains, over some ridges of yet undissolved snow. I was fortunate in my companion. Dr. Rink never seemed at a loss; he had a ready and instructive answer to all my questions, whether they related to flowers, minerals, or the physical condition of the country.

Climbing to the top of the first hill, we took a survey of the district; wild and rugged in the extreme, the whole interior visible from the point where we stood appeared to consist of mountains with intervening winding passages—I cannot call them valleys, for our idea of a valley is connected with verdure and softened beauty, while these passes are covered with blocks of stones and boulders, very few flowers interspersed among them, and those apparently pleading for life. We were happy enough to obtain a few minerals, some specimens of rough garnets, allanite, tantalite, molybdenite, &c., with copper, tin, and iron ores in small quantities.

Passing round the corner of one of the huge blocks which bestrewed our way, we startled a couple of hares quietly feeding at its base; they scampered off some distance before one of them fell at the discharge of my gun. At that season it did not differ in appearance and colour from the hares of this country, but its coat becomes completely white in the winter time, giving it a greater chance of escape from its enemies; it is then generally traced by its footprints, an Eskimo being able to distinguish by the shape and feeling of these whether the track has been made days, hours, or minutes before.

As the spring advances after the long winter, they are

THE INTERIOR IN SUMMER.

often found sitting at the corner of a stone, intently gazing at the sun.

We found a pretty good sprinkling of flowers during our ramble: a species of buttercup was occasionally seen in the marshy plain behind the settlement; a variety of poppy, with its large yellow flower, looking like a sickly child with an overgrown head, peeped out from under the shelter of a piece of rock; while the Alpine stitchwort occasionally showed itself, reminding me of the common flower in our own hedges. In some few favoured places the hill-sides would be covered with the purple saxifrage, while still more rarely specimens of other species of this Alpine genus of flowers were obtained. In one sequestered nook my eye was delighted with the sight of a violet and a campanula in cordial juxtaposition, and the presence of a dandelion and an alchemilla almost induced the idea that I was on a Scotch mountain, among civilised people, rather than among glaciers and Eskimos.

The most ambitious growth here was that of beech and willow bushes, eighteen or twenty inches high, having stems about the thickness of a man's thumb. These are gathered by the natives as firewood for the winter in the Danish houses.

As we continued our walk we came to the edge of a small lake, on the far corner of which some ducks were quietly floating. By a series of manœuvres, the chief of which consisted in almost breaking one's back by stooping, we crawled from behind one block to the next, and succeeded in getting within shot, when we obtained a couple of brace.

On our way back to the ship a thick fog came on, and had it not been that my companion was well acquainted with the country we should have been at a loss to find our way, as scarcely a landmark was visible. When we got on board and changed our clothes, we felt quite ready for dinner.

Our conversation was at first limited to an interchange of looks and gestures, as only one of our party understood Danish thoroughly. Dr. Rink, however, speaking English fluently, by the additional aid of French and German, we contrived after a time to be quite a voluble party. It was amusing to hear the disjointed sentences at one end of the table commenced in German and eked out with French at the other, the *patois* consisting of an alternation of English and Danish.

After coffee we went on shore, where we found our men had preceded us, and were showing their gallantry to the Eskimo young ladies. The sound of the fiddle attracted us to a very small ball-room, twenty-five feet square, where from sixty to eighty people had managed to crowd themselves, and were dancing to their hearts' content. The drapery of the ladies not requiring much extra space, it was marvellous to see the ease with which they glided in and out of this close-packed assemblage, always keeping time to the music, which consisted of two violins, a flute, and a tub-end covered over with seal-skin, serving as drum for the nonce.

One of the sailors had elected himself master of the ceremonies, and, seated in the window, endeavoured to keep proper order, greatly to the detriment of the room, it must be admitted. This had evidently not been cleaned since the last stock of blubber-casks and sealskins had left it; and filled with this crowd of not very cleanly persons, going through the exciting exercise of a sailor's reel or an Eskimo dance, with only the door and one window as ventilators, the effect may be imagined when the latter was obstructed by the major-domo.

A glance in was quite sufficient for us, and we pro-

SEAL-HUNTING ON ICE-FIELDS.

ceeded to have a look at the different "buildings" of which the settlement consists. The principal are the governor's house and the neat little wooden Lutheran church, which boasted its belfry and organ, and had seats for some 150 people. Close down to the water's edge was the storehouse, in which the fruits of the last winter's hunt were deposited, consisting of seal and reindeer skins, blubber, &c., to the value of about 15,000 dollars. Then there is the import storehouse, where a miscellaneous assortment of articles—biscuit, blankets, and bullet-moulds; stockings, shot, sugar, and stew-pans; rice, rifles, and ropes, &c.—were to be found in incongruous proximity. Currency consists of paper notes, printed in Copenhagen, which become valuable on their arrival in Greenland, little silver money changing hands.

After seeing the different piles of goods stowed away in these buildings, we turned our attention to the exterior of the dwellings of the Eskimo. Round one of them were grouped a number of natives, talking in a slow, hesitating way; one of them seemed from his looks to be rather irate, but the easy manner in which he allowed his words to gurgle out of his throat would not have led any one to suppose that he was otherwise than at peace with all mankind.

The interesting operation of cutting up a seal, which had just been brought in, was going on inside one of the huts; the dainty bits, such as the liver, &c., were taken possession of by the favoured ones of the household, to be cooked over the stone blubber-lamp. A couple of old dames were entertaining each other over a cup of coffee, which luxurious beverage was the first-fruits of the seal-skin just deposited in the store.

Heartily tired after my day's ramble, I joyfully turned in for the night.

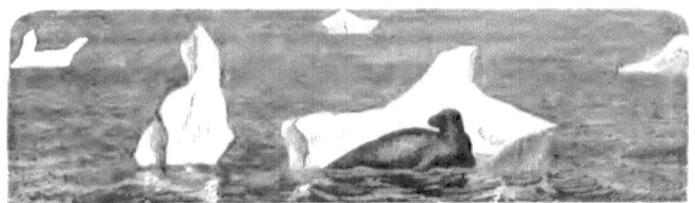

GREENLAND.

CHAPTER III.

HOLSTEINBORG.

ON the 28th of April we made the land near Holsteinborg; not being aware of the exact position of the settlement, we kept along the coast to avoid the numerous shoals and sunken rocks. Being early in the season, the latter were topped by sea-ice of considerable thickness, which was somewhat an aid to us in finding out their position; but being similar in appearance to small pieces of ordinary floating ice, they were often mistaken for it, to the great risk and danger of the ship. We passed many icebergs aground near the off-lying islands.

The afternoon being thick and foggy, as it often is in spring in Greenland, and a native who had been out seal-hunting in his kajak coming alongside, with the bight of a rope at either end of the kajak, he and it were brought on board. Being acquainted with the coast-line even in a fog, he piloted the ship in and out of the island passages as easily as if she had been his own canoe.

Presently the sun burst through the clouds for a while, dissipating the mist, and affording us a peep of the coast along which we were creeping. Occasionally we passed the mouth of one of those wondrous fiords, the sight of which would alone repay a visit to the north ; its deep and placid waters winding inland amid every variety of scenery and colouring of which these grim Arctic regions are capable, or we coasted under cliffs some thousand feet high with their miniature glaciers between rocks of gneiss ; the stillness of the uninhabited land, the smooth clear water, the ship stealing along with nothing to break the solemn silence, save the plunge of the seaman's lead or the flap of some wild-fowl passing us, while the awe of our silence was intensified by the constant fear of being overwhelmed by an avalanche.

Our pilot soon left us, as he had some distance to go before he reached his home. Scarcely were we left alone before it began to snow ; the fog came down again from off the land ; again we had to grope our way.

Fortunately other Eskimos had been out hunting ; two of whom came on board and piloted us between the islands to the sheltered bay, at the head of which the settlement stands, just outside which the assistant factor came alongside with a boat's crew, the coxswain taking the ship in to her berth, where we let go in seventeen fathoms, mooring her to the rocks with bow and stern hawsers.

The natives in their kajaks at once crowded round the ship; fastening their frail canoes together with pieces of seal line, numbers of them came on board, and showed, by hauling on the hawsers, ropes, &c., that they would willingly do us a kindness. When the deck was cleared, and all the ropes coiled down, an immediate barter was set up between the sailors and the natives; seal-skin boots,

DANISH SETTLEMENT AT HOLSTEINBORG.

trousers, and jumpers soon changed hands, and many an old jacket, &c., went on shore. The greatest demand among the young ladies was for silk handkerchiefs, which they used as head bandages, and their triumph was considerable when one of them became the happy possessor of so rare and prized an article; as there were but few on board available for barter, they were soon at a high premium.

Being early in the season, there was some little night; consequently the ship's deck was deserted soon after ten o'clock by all except the quartermaster of the watch. The next morning was bright and lovely, with a pleasant breeze off the land; the harbour in which we lay was well land-locked, so that we were secure from any of those williewaws so frequent in the fiords of this coast. Snow lay thickly over all the land, the summer sun having only denuded the surface of a few rocks; the houses of the settlement having a coating of black tar, had almost entirely thrown off their winter covering, and stood out well on the white background. The little chapel, with its heaven-pointing turret, was buried on all sides in snow, the windows and doors being the only spots free from it; a deep pathway, with a four-foot bank of snow on either side, formed the approach to this house of God.

As the evening closed in, the sight of the setting sun was splendid. Close to us was the arm of a fiord, at the upper end of which, as if wedged in between the rocks, the sun was sinking. The few clouds immediately above were of a deep golden hue, in striking contrast with the dark purple of those some distance beyond; the rays reflected from white snow, dark rock, and blue water gave innumerable and gorgeous tints; the moon came peeping over an adjoining headland; the rocks were mirrored in the water, which seemed rising to kiss the golden sunbeams; our boat lay idly by the shore; and it was only when the low quack of a coming flock of ducks brought us back to material things that we were reminded that the game-bag was not yet full.

The next day being Sunday, we had, as usual, divine service on the lower deck, after which I went on shore, as the sound of the bell told that the time for service approached.

> "It was a little church, and plain, almost
> To ugliness, yet lacking not its charm."

Groups of Eskimo women and children were walking quietly thither as I landed, and, when I reached it, it was almost full.

After dinner, taking a walk over the rocks, I had a fine view of the sea and its countless islands. It was indeed a lovely maritime landscape, out of the power of better pencils than mine to depict. In the evening there was a halo round the sun—that is, a circle of light 45° in diameter, with the sun for a centre, and the mock sun on either side, on a plane passing horizontally through it. This phenomenon is dependent on the reflection of the solar rays from small snow crystals, with which the air is often loaded in these northern climes.

Returning from my walk late, I remained on shore, and supped with the governor. The priest, his wife, and the two assistants joined us. We partook of an excellent repast, consisting of venison, dried salmon, ptarmigan, and other delicacies, which seemed strangely out of place in this secluded spot.

156   GREENLAND.

As I proceeded to my boat, the Eskimo dogs whi(
were there collected made the night hideous by bayi(
the moon, the coming gale seeming to have stirred (
their innate powers of howling. Seaward all look(
black, even our vessel, whose tall masts pointing heave(

THE HALO.

wards, seemed to invite the storm. On Monday it ble(
half a gale all day, and snowed constantly. It w(
miserably cold, so that I did not leave the ship, exce(
for a couple of hours to sit with the governor. (

Tuesday there was only a gentle breeze from the northward, and scarcely a cloud to be seen.

> "Blue, sunny sky above; below,
> A blue and sunny sea;
> A world of blue, wherein did blow
> One soft wind steadily."

An iceberg, about 160 feet high, had come into the harbour during the night, and gleamed brightly against the dark rocks. I again ascended a neighbouring mountain, and, from an elevation of 1,800 to 2,000 feet, had a good panoramic view. As the sun reached its highest, and seemed to rest before it declined, the same formed a splendid picture. The hues of silver frost, purple and neutral, would have enchanted a painter, while the hopelessness of any attempt to catch them, and transfer their fleeting beauty to his canvas, would well-nigh have broken his heart.

In the evening I visited the carcases of three whales, which, having been denuded of their blubber, lay stranded on the shore, and served as banqueting-rooms for the Eskimo dogs. These were so satiated with their repast, they could hardly screw up their tails upon their backs—their way of manifesting pleased recognition—but lay alongside the scene of their enjoyment, smiling benignly, and unable to move.

Our approach frightened away some half-dozen ravens, which had been attracted by the carrion lying at our feet. These birds are found very far north; I remember seeing two in the middle of January, at a temperature of —50°, flying as leisurely as if it had been the hottest day experienced by any of their species. These same birds built their nest and bred in lat. 72° N., showing an instance of a bird which breeds both in arctic and tropico-temperate climates. Those which we now disturbed from their feast flew lazily away, and settled on a rock a few yards from us, evidently looking upon us as intruders, and patiently waiting our departure.

A few words about the Eskimo dog, which has been here mentioned for the first time. This animal, whose services are indispensable to the inhabitants of Northern Greenland, is not unlike our shepherd's dog in its general aspect, but is more muscular, and has a broader chest, owing, in a great measure, to the hard work it is inured to. The ears are pointed, and, with its long muzzle, serve to increase the wolfishness of its appearance. An ordinary well-grown dog will be somewhat smaller than a Newfoundland dog, but broad, like a mastiff. The coat of this dog consists of long hair, and in the winter it is further protected by a soft, downy under-covering, which does not appear during the warm weather.

Their education begins at a very early age. When about two months old, eight or ten puppies are harnessed to a sledge with two experienced runners, and by means of frequent and cruel beatings, and angry repetitions of their names, they are **taught their** duty, but not without **much** hard labour on the driver's part, and great patience. Personal experience **has** taught me some of the peculiar **difficulties of** managing a puppy-dog team.

Each dog is harnessed to a separate line; and these, being about eight abreast, fully endowed with all—and more than all—the playfulness of young animals in this country, the effect may be pictured when, all jumping on each other in most admired confusion, the lines become entangled, and are only set right after many efforts. This process has to be repeated again and again, as the gambols or quarrels of the young dogs render it necessary.

The whip, too, would puzzle a London cabby, and is not

THE DOG-SLEDGE.

easy for a novice to use—a lash from twenty to twenty-four feet long, attached to a handle *one* foot long; it requires no small amount of dexterity to avoid wounding your own person in an attempt to make an example of one of your pupils. When trained, however, they are guided only by a touch of the whip to the near or off leader, and over smooth ice, with a light load, can be made to go seven or eight miles per hour.

GREENLAND.

CHAPTER IV.

GODHAVEN.

THE voyage from Holsteinborg to Godhaven was rather tedious. Being prevented by fog and ice from at once reaching our destination, I was enabled to dredge, and procured a considerable variety of treasures—starfishes, holothurias, crustacea, annelids, and shells.

On the evening of the 10th May we had hoped to be in port, but our wishes were not realised, and we were in much danger. At one time we were startled by finding the end of one of the Kron Prins Islands right under our bow. We had not much time to make our escape, being hardly more than half the ship's length off before perceiving our perilous position. At another time we found ourselves within forty yards of a formidable iceberg, which the fog had hindered our seeing.

For six days we were detained at the Whalefish Islands; but on the 17th May we at last anchored close to the settlement of Godhaven, the seat of the Northern Inspectorate of Greenland. It is situated on a spur of metamorphic rock, which juts out in a peninsular form from Disco Island, the mainland of which is composed of trap or basalt of recent igneous origin. These rocks reach the height of 3,000, 4,000, or even 5,000 feet, and are, in some places, formed into pillars, in a manner which may be imagined by those who have visited Staffa or the Giant's Causeway.

The situation is singularly beautiful, with its beetling cliff of dark rock, like the turrets of some giant fortification, stretching darkly before the traveller, and presenting the same aspect from seaward—inaccessible, inhabited only by sea-birds, such as guillemots, loons, ducks, gulls, &c.

It was not till 1721 that any attempt was made to ascertain the religious condition of the Eskimos, or to Christianize them.

The "wild" Eskimos of the Arctic regions believe in the existence of two great and a number of inferior spirits. The chief of these, "Tongarsuk," the great spirit, is supposed to give power to the "angerkok," or priest, who is the medium of communication between him and the people, by whom he is only known by name, which is never mentioned without becoming reverence.

This great spirit is supposed to assume different forms, —at one time that of a man, at another that of a bear,

M

while often he is spoken of as purely spirit. The other great spirit, supposed to be the principle of evil, is represented as a female, but has no name.

The angerkoks profess, by means of their familiar spirit, to charm away bad luck from the hunter, to change the weather, or to heal the sick. The lesser spirits are believed to control the different elements, and from their ranks Tongarsuk selects the familiars for the priests. One of these lesser spirits, who rules the air, is supposed to be so vicious, that the Eskimos are loath to stir out after dark for fear of offending him.

They suppose the sun and moon to be brother and sister, who having quarrelled, the sun bit off one of his sister's breasts; and the maimed appearance presented by the moon is caused by her turning her wounded side to the earth. The aurora borealis is supposed to be the game of "hockey," played by the departed spirits of their friends and relatives.

Now, however, owing to the unwearied labours of missionaries in Danish Greenland, I believe, there is not one heathen remaining. A few customs, which are followed more from habit than belief, however, remain, though these are not more absurd than many which obtain in any country district in Great Britian or Ireland.

In Smith Sound, and on the western shores of Baffin's Bay or Davis' Strait, the Eskimos are yet in the darkness of heathenism, and there are many "angerkoks" who believe all the superstitions I have mentioned.

From incidental reference to the social life of the

GODHAVEN.   165

Greenlanders, some idea will have been already gained of its nature. Filthy in his person and habits, and regardless of the amenities of civilised life, yet the Eskimo is not a *savage*, being possessed of a certain negative amiability of nature which would prevent his being placed in that category. On the whole, he behaves well in his

HUNTING THE SEAL.

social relations, is a moderately affectionate son, husband, and father.

The occupation of the Eskimos, though substantially the same throughout Greenland, differs somewhat according to the latitude.

In South Greenland, it is seal-hunting and cod-fishing.

Seated in his kajak, with his spear alongside, his coil of line in front, his seal-skin buoy behind, two bird-spears on the upper part of the canoe, and his rifle inside, the hunter takes his departure, putting on a white calico jumper over his sealskin, if he be likely to meet with ice.

Paddle in hand, and gliding through the water at six miles per hour, he soon sees a seal's head above the surface. Cautiously getting his spear ready, as he rests on his paddle, and clearing his line, he quietly follows in the track of the animal, whose keenness of hearing obliges him to be as noiseless as possible. Arrived within proper distance, he launches the spear, which, striking the seal, leaves the harpoon-head sticking, and away go line, buoy, and prey. The buoy prevents the seal from sinking too low, or swimming to any distance. If the wound be not fatal, the animal quickly rises to the surface to breathe, and, the spot being indicated by the buoy, the ready hunter, adroitly darting another spear, ultimately succeeds in his object. It is then hauled on the top of the kajak, or fastened alongside.

The hunter then generally returns to his home, content with killing one; but should he meet with any piece of floating ice, knowing the propensity of the seal to bask and rest on these, he paddles up to them. The white jumper now stands him in good stead. The animal, aroused by the plashing of the paddle, rises on its hind flippers, gazes with its large, lustrous eyes at the kajak; seeing the white surface, mistakes it for a piece of ice, and resumes its former position. The hunter, now balances himself as well as possible, and, taking a good aim, fires, often killing the seal, but occasionally missing his aim.

THE WALRUS.

In Middle Greenland, the Eskimos add the pursuit of the deer, in the spring and autumn, to the two descriptions of hunting mentioned above. The hunters resort to the passes and valleys frequented by the deer; then, lying in wait for the herd, they single out their game, and either get it at once, or, wounding it, stalk as is done in Scotland. The numbers which are daily destroyed in this manner, during the season, are so great, that the natives often do not encumber themselves with anything but the skin and the tongue, the latter being considered a delicacy; they leave the bodies to go to waste. At times, however, the deer are very scarce.

In North Greenland, besides seal-hunting and deer-stalking, the Eskimos are occasionally engaged in the chase of the walrus and the narwhal (or sea-unicorn); but as the danger is great, the natives are loath to attack either single-handed. In one of the settlements I met a man whose brother, having harpooned a walrus, was at once turned upon by the infuriated beast, who, in the sight of my informant, struck him in the back with his tusks, and killed him at one blow. This same man had another brother drowned in his kajak, after having harpooned a walrus. The line not being clear, the animal, in sinking, dragged the canoe under water.

Sometimes a gale off the land springs up whilst the hunter is out at sea. His only chance then is to make for the nearest ice, and hauling his canoe upon it, to drift with it till the gale be over. This ice has at times, though rarely, drifted more than half way across Davis' Straits.

ORKNEY.

ORKNEY.

CHAPTER I.

SCENERY OF THE GROUP.

THE islands of Orkney and Shetland are so little known that many persons, in other respects well informed, seem to look upon them as a collection of rocks either uninhabitable or inhabited by a race of men almost as untamed as the seals which play upon their shores, and with intellects little more developed; a race with whom the civilised world has no communion, living on fish, dressing in sealskin, gloriously ignorant of civilization, destitute of education. But these northern islands and their inhabitants are in reality very interesting, and it is in the hope of making them better known and appreciated that I now attempt to give some account of the nearer group—the Orkneys.

Separated from the mainland by the Pentland Frith,

from ten to twelve miles in width, and "confronting" (as Mr. Balfour, their latest historian, remarks), within a few hours' sail, the mouths of the Baltic and the Elbe; indented with fine harbours, easily made as impregnable as any in Northern Europe, and never boomed like them by half a year of ice; with a soil of more than ordinary fertility; and a sea-loving people, hardy, intelligent, and enterprising—Orkney was well adapted to become the vanguard of northern civilization and commerce."

The Orkney Islands are upwards of sixty in number, containing from 400,000 to 500,000 acres, and a population of 32,416, according to the census of 1861. Twenty-five are inhabited, and to these only the name of *island* is generally given. Those not inhabited, and used only for pasture, are called *holms*.

The general appearance of the group is flat, and to some extent tame. The only very high hill is Hoy Head, which is upwards of 1,800 feet above the level of the sea.

No trees meet the eye. You must look for them in some sheltered spot under the protecting care of a large building. In some of the islands attempts are being made to foster them, but with little prospect of success; in others again there is not as much wood growing as would make a walking-stick.

Orkney must have undergone a most remarkable change in respect to climate, for in the mosses trunks of very large trees are found; and I have seen many deer's horns that have been dug up, proving that in some prehistoric age this now treeless, deerless country had not only deer but forests to shelter them.

The mosses containing these remains—trees, deer's horns, and hazel nuts—extend under the present sea level; and at very low tides they are sometimes exposed, as in Otterwick Bay, Sanday, and Deerness.

Pomona, or Mainland, is by far the largest of the Orkney group; its length from east to west is upwards of thirty miles, and its breadth in some places from six to eight miles. The two largest towns of Orkney are in Pomona—Stromness, in the south-west, with a population of about 3,000, and a very fine harbour; and Kirkwall, the capital of Orkney, which lies on the north side, and contains above 4,000 inhabitants, many good shops, three banks, two newspapers, churches and schools in proportion to the population.

The principal street is about a mile in length, and is made up of houses that would not seem out of place in any county town. It is not surprising that the metropolis of Orkney should now contain all the necessaries, and most of the luxuries, which modern refinement demands; but it is strange to find that seven hundred years ago, on this extreme verge of civilisation, and so near the polar regions, there arose a cathedral, more perfect, very little smaller, and in some respects finer, than that of Glasgow.

Near the cathedral are the ruins of the bishop's palace. Within an easy walk from Kirkwall is Wideford Hill from the top of which nearly all the islands may be seen;

and no one who goes there on a clear day will hesitate to admit that the scene before him, looking seaward, is one of exquisite beauty.

In calm weather, the sea, land-locked by the islands, resembles a vast lake, clear and bright as a mirror, and without a ripple save from the gentle impulse of the tide. Here, a bluff headland stands out in bold relief against the horizon; there, the more distant islet is lost in sea and sky; on one side a shelving rock sends out a black tongue-like point, sharp as a needle, losing itself in the water, where it forms one of those reefs so common among the islands, and so fatal to strangers, but which every Orkney boatman knows as we do the streets of our native town; while on the other side a green holm, covered with cattle and ponies, slopes gently to the water's edge.

Then there is the dovetailing and intercrossing of one point with another, the purple tints of the islands, the deep blue of the sea, the indentations of the coast, the boats plying their oars or lingering lazily on the waters, the white sails of the pleasure yachts contrasting with the dark brown canvas of the fishing craft, and here and there a large merchant vessel entering or leaving the harbour;—all these combine to make a most lovely picture, in which the additional ornament of trees is not missed.

And again, in a storm, the boiling tides, the green and white billows, the pillars of foam which spout aloft when dashed against the rocks, make a scene with which the absence of trees is in perfect harmony. You feel that trees here would be out of their element. In calm weather they are not needed, in a storm they would seem out of place.

Any one who has seen an Orkney sunset in June or July, tracing its diamond path across island, reef, and tideway, must confess that it is scarcely possible to suggest an addition to its beauty.

THE STENNIS STONES.

From Wideford Hill you can cast your eye upon structures that are memorials of every form of religion that has ever existed in Scotland. Stennis and its standing stones are in sight, eight or ten miles off. Nearer to you are some of those inscrutable mounds called Picts' houses. On the Isle of Eagleshay, which may be seen from the same spot, stand the walls and tower of probably the earliest Christian church in Britain.

The Standing Stones of Stennis are still about thirty in number, forming portions of two circles, the larger of which measures above a hundred yards in diameter, and the smaller about thirty-four. These circles are not now complete, as many of the stones have fallen and many have disappeared, but sufficient traces remain to show what they were. The stones vary in form and size, and are all totally unhewn. The largest is about fourteen feet high, but the average height is from eight to ten. They are grand, solemn-looking old veterans, painfully silent regarding their past life, as if ashamed to speak of those bloody rites in which they may have had a share.

They were formerly called *Druidical Circles*, perhaps for no better reason than that their history is utterly unknown.

Of the mounds called Picts' houses, of which there are hundreds in Orkney, we know as little as we do of the stones, save that they are of two kinds, very similar in construction, and that the smaller seem to have been the dwellings of the early inhabitants of the country, and the others the sepulchres of their dead. These structures are not strictly subterranean, although they are covered with earth. They were either erected on level ground, or excavated in the side of a hill. They are built of large stones converging towards the centre, where an aperture seems to have been left for air and light. Bones and teeth of the horse, cow, sheep, and boar were found in the Picts' houses on Wideford Hill opened in 1849.

The climate of Orkney is moist and mild; there are neither such warm summers nor such cold winters as in

A PICTS' HOUSE.

the south and west of Scotland. A gentleman who has lived in Orkney the greater part of his life told me that he had seldom seen ice strong enough to bear a man's weight. The Gulf Stream is, no doubt, the cause of this.

The length of daylight makes these islands a desirable summer residence. I have myself read a newspaper without difficulty at midnight in the month of June; and I have been told by a friend who lives in Orkney, that on the shortest day he has read the *Times* at four o'clock P.M. by daylight, or rather by the beautiful twilight of that region, for in winter the sun is only about four hours above the horizon.

The soil is in many parts mossy, but there is almost everywhere a stiff clay underneath, and this, when ploughed up, and mixed with the moss, makes a very good loam. In many places, the ground merely requires to be "tickled with the plough, that it may smile with the harvest," as somebody has said.

There is, perhaps, no district in Scotland where so much is being done in the way of improving the land. In 1814, very considerable progress had been made on some of the larger estates in Orkney, more especially in the North Isles, where turnips were pretty extensively grown, and at least one flock of fine Cheviot merino sheep was profitably kept; but it was not until about twenty-five years ago that the agricultural movement began in earnest.

Previous to that time, the sea had been the sole support of the working man. He rented land, and paid his rent out of fish and seaweed. The women were generally the farmers, while the men fished.

It is not many years since Orkney made out of her seaweed alone an annual income of 15,000*l.*, 20,000*l.*, and even 25,000*l*. There is a kind of seaweed, the *fucus palmatus*, commonly called tangle, thrown up in great abundance on the shores of the Orkneys, and also of the Western Isles. From this a substance called kelp is made, valuable from the large amount of iodine it contains, and once extensively used in the manufacture of soap and glass.

The process of kelp-making is as follows:—The seaweed is collected and dried, and put into a hole in the ground about three feet wide. A live coal is then put in, and the heap is allowed to smoulder. During the smouldering it is stirred with an iron-hook, until in course of time it gets into a state somewhat like molten lead. When it cools and dries, it is kelp. Besides iodine, it contains glauber salts, common salt, and carbonate of soda.

The thriftlessness of the farming of past days is well illustrated by an anecdote I had from Mr. Balfour, the proprietor. His father, observing that one of his tenants was always in difficulties, though he did not pay a farthing of rent, said to him one day, that he was surprised at his being so much in want, seeing that he had a good croft, and paid nothing for it.

"Oh, Captain Balfour," he replied, "I *due* pay a rent."

"Why, what rent do you pay?"

"Weel—I *sud* pay a hen."

Shapinshay is now in a very satisfactory state of cultivation, about 5,000 acres being under the plough, although the rental is as yet only about 1,500*l*. A dozen years ago it imported meal for the support of its inhabitants; it now exports largely grain, potatoes, cattle, sheep, pigs, eggs, &c.

The habits and mode of life of the islanders were very primitive even fifty years ago. The chimney of the cottage was simply a hole in the roof, and the fire was in the middle of the floor, so that the smoke had to find its way out as best it might. Such fire-places have, I think, almost disappeared from Orkney, at least I do not remember seeing one.

In old times the islanders had many strange beliefs and antipathies, which some of the older people still cherish. For instance, they have a prejudice against turbot, and will not eat it—nor even name it at sea—although they constantly eat halibut, a much less delicate fish of the same species.

A strange belief was held generally at one time that drowned persons are changed into seals. The island of Borey in the Bay of Milburn, is sometimes called the Seal Island, and a romantic legend is told in connection with it, which has already found its way into print, but not so fully as it was related to me.

It was a fine summer evening, and Harold of the isle of Gairsay had been fishing till late, when, as the sun went down, he heard the most enchanting music. He followed the sound till he reached the island of Borey, where he saw a company of gaily-dressed people dancing to it, but no musicians were visible. He went close inshore, and saw a number of black objects like beasts. They lay so still that he landed and took up one, and found it to be a seal-skin. He watched the dancers for some time, and when the sun began to rise the music suddenly ceased, and they all hurried down to the shore. Harold dropped the seal-skin into his boat, pushed off, and pulled away to a short distance, to see what would happen next. Each person seized a seal-skin, put it on, and plunged into the sea.

One woman alone was left, and she went along the shore seeking the seal-skin which Harold had taken. He put back to the island, spoke to her, and then recognised her as his own mother, who had been drowned many years before. She told him that all drowned persons became seals, and once a month they were allowed to resume their human form and come on shore at sunset, and dance till sunrise. She begged hard for her seal-skin, which at first he refused to give up; but on her promising that he should have the prettiest maiden in all Seal-land for his wife, he gave it back. She desired him to return to Borey that day month: she would then show him the seal-skin of the girl who should be his bride, and he was to keep the skin carefully hidden from the owner, whom he would thus have in his own power.

On the night appointed Harold went again to Borey; again he heard the beautiful music, and saw the mysterious dancers. His mother went to the shore and laid her hand on a seal-skin, which Harold put into his boat, then rowed home and concealed it. Before sunrise he returned to Borey. The music ceased as before, the dancers resumed their seal-skins, and disappeared in the sea—all but one beautiful girl, who went about wringing her hands and weeping for the loss of hers.

After a little time Harold approached and spoke to her. She told him that she was the daughter of a pagan king. He endeavoured to comfort her, and succeeded so well, that she consented to go home with him and become his wife. He loved her fondly, and she bore him several children; but at length she fell sick—some secret grief was consuming her. Often she asked for her seal-skin, but Harold never suffered her to see it; and at last she confessed that she was anxious about her soul. A priest was sent for, and she was baptized; yet still she was not satisfied, and pined away.

"Harold," she said one day, "we have lived long and happily together. If we part, we part for ever. If I die, you cannot be sure that my soul is saved, for I have long lived a pagan. To-night is the dancing night; roll me in my seal-skin and leave me on the beach; they cannot take me away if I am a Christian. But you must go out of sight, and return for me in the morning; then you will know my fate."

Harold yielded to her wish. He laid her on the shore, and went himself to the other side of Gairsay to wait till sunrise. All night he sat with his face buried in his hands. Once he heard a sudden wail; they had found his wife on the shore, but he dared not move. That short midsummer night seemed endless to him; at last the sun appeared, and he hastened to the place where he had left her. She was still there. They had not taken her away, for she was a Christian. She was dead, but with a smile on her face that spoke of a soul at peace. That smile comforted Harold, and assured him that their parting would not be for ever.

ORKNEY.

CHAPTER II.

OCCUPATION OF THE PEOPLE.

THE islanders are brave and hardy. During the season of egg-gathering they may be seen at one time climbing a precipice to rob the nests, at another swinging from the face of a rock with nothing between them and almost certain death but a rope round their waists.

They thus naturally acquire the habit of talking of danger and even of death in a way that seems to indicate indifference to both. Probably few, however, reach the degree of coolness exhibited by an old man who went out one day with his son to gather eggs. The son descended the face of a high rock with one end of a rope round his waist, the other being fastened to a stake above, while the old man remained in his boat at the base, in case of accident. The precaution was not unnecessary, for the rope gave way, and the lad fell into the sea. There was a considerable ground swell, and the poor boy had sunk once or twice before his father could rescue him, but at last he was taken into the boat almost lifeless. This elicited from the father the simple remark, "Eh! I'm thinking thou's wat, Tam."

The saying that those born to be hanged will never be drowned, is probably no truer of hanging than of other deaths. Tam was reserved for a different but scarcely less enviable fate. An acquaintance of the old man's, years afterwards, reminded him of Tam's escape, and asked him what had become of him, to which the father replied in the same indifferent tone: "Tam? our Tam? Oh! Tam gaed awa' to a far country, and the haithens ate him."

This anecdote I know to be perfectly true, and I have as reliable authority for another of the same kind.

A man was one day gathering eggs on the face of a precipitous rock, and while creeping cautiously yet fearlessly along a ledge little broader than the sole of his foot, he came to an angle round which he must pass. The wall-like steepness of the rock and the narrowness of the ledge made this under any circumstances difficult and dangerous. The difficulty, however, grew into an apparent impossibility, when he found on reaching the corner that he had the wrong foot first. To turn back was impossible, to get round while his feet were in that position was equally so.

The danger was observed by the friend who related the

occurrence to me, and who looked on with terror at the probable consequences, for a false step or a stumble involved certain death. The man paused for a moment, took off his broad bonnet, in which he carried, as was customary, his snuff-horn, and after shaking up the snuff in the most unconcerned way, he took three hearty pinches, and then returned the horn to his bonnet, and the bonnet to his head. Then straightening himself up, he made an agile spring, and got the right foot first.

It was an awful moment for the looker-on, and an awful risk for the performer. Happily it was successful; he got round the point, and finally reached the top of the rock in safety.

My friend, who had waited for his ascent, said to him: "Man, Johnnie, were ye no feared?"

"Eh man, if I had been feared, I wudna be here."

"I dare say that," replied my friend; "but what made you think of taking a snuff when you were in such danger?"

"Weel," he answered, with admirable simplicity and truth, "I thocht I was needin't."

It is impossible, within the limits of a short paper, to give a detailed description of the various islands. Nor is this necessary.

I cannot, however, omit giving some account of North Ronaldshay, the most curious, most primitive, and most remote of the whole group. It is also the most difficult of access. Perhaps I was unusually unlucky, but I made five several attempts to reach it without success.

EGG-GATHERING.

In my sixth attempt, however, three years ago, I was more fortunate, though even then it was with some difficulty. The frith between North Ronaldshay and Sanday is a very dangerous one, and the wind and tide must be carefully consulted. If you start too late to reach it before the turn of the tide, you are almost inevitably carried back to your starting point, unless the wind be all the more favourable.

A friend of mine, with his wife and some ladies, had once got within gun-shot of the shore as the tide turned, when, caught in the fringe of it, they were carried off as in a mill-stream, and in a very short time were miles off.

It is very flat, the highest elevation being only 47 feet. What strikes one at first sight as most peculiar, is a dry stone wall, between five and six feet high, with small holes left at regular intervals. It stretches along the beach as far as you can see, and is but a little above high-water mark. You are still more surprised to learn that it goes right round the island.

The purpose of this wall is very puzzling to a stranger. The island is a small one, only 4,000 acres. Can it be meant to keep the young islanders from tumbling into the sea? or, if they are supposed to have more sense, is it to keep the sheep from the shore, lest they should be swept off by the waves which often play wildly there? No, but exactly the reverse.

The wall was built for the double purpose of depriving the winds as they pass through it of the saline vapour which used to blight the crops, and of keeping the sheep out. The grass is very valuable, being required for the cattle, so the sheep must have other fare. What other fare, we naturally ask, can a sheep have than grass? Seaweed—nothing but seaweed.

The sheep here are unlike any animals of the species I ever saw. They are called wild sheep, are lean and scraggy, and are like goats. Their mutton is dark coloured. The natives like it very much, and some people say it has the flavour of venison. The taste is certainly peculiar, and suggests the idea of seaweed.

Almost every rood of the island is under cultivation. There are therefore no peats, and there is no wood, except when an unfortunate ship is wrecked. Coals and peats are very expensive. To obtain a supply of fuel, the people have recourse to an expedient practised by the Arabs in the desert, and also by the inhabitants of Cornwall.

Every family has a cow, and when the byre is cleaned out, the dung heap, instead of being used for agricultural purposes, is mixed with straw, and then cut into pieces, which are called scones. These are laid in the sun to dry, and are not used until they are a year old, when the sulphuretted hydrogen is gone, and the smell in burning is not so offensive. One can see from this why the cow is made so much of, and has the grass all to herself, to the detriment of the sheep. It is not every animal that can supply us with meat, drink, clothing, and fire. It is scarcely necessary to say, that the atmosphere of houses heated by this kind of fuel is not particularly pleasant.

OCCUPATION OF THE PEOPLE. 191

When I saw some smoked fish hanging in a cottage, I could not help asking if they had been smoked with scones.

"Oh, yes!"

"But does it not spoil the fish?"

"Well, peat or wood is better, but we soon get used to it."

AN ORKNEY FARMHOUSE.

I could not help thinking that this eel-like facility in getting "used" to things is very fortunate, and that it is the same kind of happy knack which discovers the flavour of venison in seaweedy mutton. The same fuel is used in Sanday, and was until lately in Papa Westray.

There is no inn on North Ronaldshay, and as the

minister was from home, I was thrown on the hospitality of a farmer, whose genuine kindness I shall not soon forget, and with whom I spent a very happy day and night. He is a very ingenious, clever fellow, who can turn his hand to anything, and do everything well. He unites in his own person the varied offices of farmer, watchmaker, smith, carpenter, kelp-maker, and, if I mistake not, doctor—in all of which capacities he is purely self-taught. He has never been further south than Kirkwall, and has no desire to leave his little world, to which he is passionately attached. He knows all about it; but his knowledge, like charity, though it begins at home, does not end there. He is thoroughly up in the politics of the day, has a keen sense of humour, is full of anecdote, and well acquainted with the works of Scott, Thackeray, and Dickens.

There is a post once a week to this island; to Westray, Sanday, and Rousay twice a week; and to some of the less remote islands once a day. This is a very different state of things from what existed formerly. At the time of the Revolution, a Scotch fisherman was imprisoned at Kirkwall, in May, 1689, for saying that King William III. had been crowned the previous November; and he was just about to be hanged for the treasonable statement when a vessel arrived to confirm it.

I have only to add one word on the people. They are, of course, first-rate sailors. In appearance there is not any very striking indication of their descent, though now and then you see a decidedly Scandinavian face. Scott describes them as known by

> "The tall form, blue eye, proportion fair,
> The limbs athletic, and the long light hair;"

and this type you not unfrequently find.

I was much struck by the exceeding gentleness of the working classes. A brawny, bearded man, who has not a particle of cowardice or sneaking in his composition, speaks to you with all the softness of a woman. Swearing is a vice from which, so far as I could judge, they are singularly free. Their language is Scotch, with some unusual words, and a slightly peculiar accent, which no doubt are the remains of the Norse. In talking to each other, the common people use the familiar and kindly "thou" instead of "you," and their bearing towards each other is gentle and pleasing.

I was one day crossing a frith in a pretty rough sea. The smack was being steered by one of the passengers, as the whole crew were required for other duties. He had a difficult task, but he managed it well, and one of the men said in banter: "Robbie, I'm thinking when thou was a young man [Robbie was not above forty] thou could steer a boat a little."

"Weel," he replied, "my han' has been oot o't for some time; but when I was a younger man and in the way o't, if onybody had said that I kent naething aboot it *I wud hae lookit at him.*"

In many other parts of Scotland the "*wud hae lookit at him*" would probably have taken an uglier form.

I have seen some pretty female faces in Orkney, but the men are generally handsomer than the women. They are a people of whom I have formed a very high opinion, both morally and intellectually. The criminal and pauper rolls of Orkney will, I believe, bear a most favourable comparison with those of any part of the kingdom.

The country presents many objects of interest to the antiquarian, the naturalist, the farmer, and the merchant. Hospitable, intelligent, industrious, and self-reliant, the Orcadians are sure to keep well abreast of their neighbours.

SHETLAND.

SHETLAND.

CHAPTER I.

LERWICK.

STARTING from Orkney, we may find some things to interest us during our eleven or twelve hours' sail.

Having got clear of the Orkneys, it is not very long till we come in sight of Fair Isle, midway between the two groups, one of the most lonely and unapproachable of human habitations, of which I shall speak more particularly by-and-by. Meanwhile, if our voyage is made by day, we shall see, as we come abreast of it, that our course is dotted over with ten or a dozen little boats, which seem in a fair way of being either run down by the steamer, or swamped by the wash of her paddles. The boatmen evidently have no such fear, for instead of avoiding the apparent danger, they pull close up, and amid the roar and rush of the steamer, which has not slackened speed, they are heard addressing the passengers hurriedly, but eargerly and clearly, with " Throw a paper throw a paper."

Such an appeal is of course irresistible to every man with a *Scotsman* in his pocket, and a particle of kindliness in his composition, and the poor Fair Isle boatmen get the benefit of both. Dozens of papers may be thrown overboard, but every one is picked up. The plunge made by the little sharp-pointed boats into the rough waters in the wake of the steamer seems perilous, and resembles nothing so much as the bobbing up and down of ducks in a very stormy pond; but the capabilities of the boats and the skill of the rowers are well known, and have been tried in many a wild sea.

This little incident causes quite a commotion on board, and those of the passengers to whom it is new are very much interested by it, and receive, I have no doubt, a livelier impression of the loneliness and isolation of that almost unvisited island than anything else could give them.

Two or three hours more and we are in Sumburgh roost, and are lucky if we escape a severe tossing. And now with Sumburgh Head in front, and the much grander Fitful Head to the left, we begin to contrast the quiet and comparatively tame beauty of Orkney with the rugged grandeur of Shetland, which for rock scenery is perhaps unsurpassed in Northern Britain.

A little further on we pass the Island of Mousa, with its famous Pictish tower, the most complete specimen of this structure in existence. It is more curious than picturesque, as may be inferred from its striking likeness to a glasswork chimney with a part of the top broken off. It is about fifty feet in diameter, and between forty and fifty feet high. It consists of two concentric walls, between which a winding stair leads up to a number of small apartmemts. The inner circular space enclosed by the walls seems to have been an open court. The use and origin of these towers, remains of which are numerous in Shetland, are uncertain. Each is said to be in sight of the other, so that intelligence of the approach of enemies might be conveyed by beacons lighted on the various summits. The peculiar shape, wide at bottom, tapering towards the middle, and again widening towards the top, seems to indicate that scaling was one mode of attack which the architect meant to guard against.

In another half-hour the steamer's gun is fired, the anchor is dropped, and you are placed face to face with the most irregular-looking town that was ever built. A stranger will not soon forget his impression on seeing Lerwick for the first time, especially if he has been taking a snooze in the saloon, and is wakened by the gun, so that its peculiarities burst full upon him at once. He sees nothing but gables, and these so huddled together in the most happy-go-lucky style, that he cannot see how locomotion through the place is possible, unless it be on the tops of the houses. The town is situated on a very steep slope, and the houses on the shore are built right down into the sea.

And now what a scramble there is at the side of the steamer! Boats by the dozen are clamouring for passengers and jostling each other in the most unceremonious way in their eagerness to get close to the steps. You get ashore somehow, though you are sure to

GIRL AND BOY OF THE BETTER CLASS.

find on landing that your luggage has come by one boat, and yourself by another. This is more annoying than at first sight appears, for every house on the shore has a pier to itself, and to join company with your luggage may thus require a long search.

On taking a walk through the town, you find that your first impression as to its irregularity was pretty correct. If one could fancy all the houses in a town of upwards of 3,000 inhabitants engaged in dancing a Scotch reel, and that just as they were going *through the reel* the music had ceased and the houses had suddenly taken root, he would form a pretty accurate impression of the plan of Lerwick. The houses, examined individually, improve on a nearer acquaintance.

Besides comfortable lodgings there is boundless hospitality. Any man with a decent coat on his back, and a fair appearance of respectability, can count not only on hearty, but, if necessary, prolonged entertainment at a Shetland fireside.

Shetland contains about a hundred islands; of these nearly thirty are inhabited, and the population is upwards of 30,000. The climate is very variable, and there is great liability to sudden and sometimes violent storms. Of this two Crimean officers had good proof a year or two ago. They paid a visit to Shetland for the purpose of shooting and fishing, and called on a friend of mine with letters of introduction. They had supplied themselves with patent pots and pans for cooking, and a portable tent, under cover of which they meant to rough it during their sojourn. My friend, who knows Shetland well, told them that none but the sappers and miners had tried the experiment, and that they had great difficulty even with their substantial house-like tent.

"Oh," said one of them, who lisped very much,

"bleth you, we've been uthed to all that thort of thing in the Crimea. We'll get on nithely, no thoubt."

They went accordingly and pitched their tent in the neighbourhood of some fishing ground, and got on pretty well for a couple of nights. During the third night, however, a gust came suddenly sweeping down the gully where they were encamped and asleep, and carried off their tent bodily, poles and all, leaving them completely *al fresco* on the ground. The tent was never more seen.

The harvest in average years is generally so late, and the weather so uncertain, that crops which promise all that could be wished to-day, are to-morrow blackened and blasted by an unexpected change to rain, sleet, or snow.

To the Shetlander the pony—by the way it is always called a horse, unless you wish to lay yourself open to the charge of speaking disparagingly—is invaluable, and yet, from the small amount of care bestowed on it, one would infer that it is not much valued. Generally, grooming is unknown, and corn an untasted luxury. He must pick up his food as best he may, at least in ordinary seasons. During snow-storms, when it is impossible for him to do so, he is supplied with some scanty fodder.

And yet what a wonderful creature he is for endurance! His height ranges from thirty to between forty and fifty inches. A pony, to whose diminutive size and apparently slender build you would think it a risk to entrust yourself, will carry you pluckily, and sometimes rapidly, over forty miles a-day of the worst roads without a stumble, and without more refreshment than half an hour's nibbling at stunted grass midway. It is a rare thing to see him with broken knees. Over shingle, bog, or quagmire, up-hill or down, leave him to himself and you are tolerably safe.

Extensive use is made of him during the annual visit of the Dutch fishermen. On these occasions the

THE FISHERMAN'S GALLOP.

more sedate walk about smoking and staring at the shop windows, while the younger seek a more exciting exercise, viz., riding on horseback. One day—mutually and immemorially agreed upon—is devoted to this. On that day dozens of those who have horses assemble, steeds in hand, on a piece of ground above the town, and thither too betake themselves the horsey portion of the Dutchmen for twopenceworth of equestrianism, which consists of a gallop out for half a mile or so and back again.

For the most part women and boys are in charge of the steeds, with every conceivable kind of halter, from the decent leather to the old and apparently rotten rope; some with saddles and stirrups, some with saddles without stirrups, some with an unambitious piece of coarse cloth or straw mat. Here a great tall fellow goes up to a very little pony, pays his twopence—it is always prepaid—and prepares to mount. But how is he to get the sabot, with a point like the prow of his own buss, into the stirrups? It evidently can't be done. Off go the sabots—a shake is all that is necessary—and he gets into the saddle.

At first he grasps only the bridle, but as the pace quickens—and it soon does that, for he means to have his twopenceworth—you see his hand slip round to the back part of the saddle and take a firm hold. This is all very well, but the saddle itself is shaky, and the pony's back short; so he must have more leverage by grasping the tail. There, now he's all right; but the motion is neither graceful nor easy, and his hat flies off. This was expected, for the woman or boy in charge follows behind for the double purpose of increasing the pace by whipping, and picking up anything that may be shaken loose.

And now that he gets toward the end of his ride, heel, bridle, and lash are pressed into service. One hand is required to hold on either by saddle or tail, the other is needed for the lash. How then can he dispose of the bridle? In his teeth of course, and there he holds it. On he comes full swing. The road is very rough and downhill now. His legs are well extended, and he is making no prehensile use of his knees. This can't last long. Hallo! there he's off rolling, with little harm done.

SHETLAND.

CHAPTER II.

FAIR ISLE AND FOULA.

ON the morning of the 4th of August we sailed from Spiggie Bay in the cutter *Nelson* on an excursion to Fair Isle and Foula. Crossing the sands we observed a great many huge backbones, and learned that they were the remains of a shoal of the bottlenose or ca'ing whales, which had stranded themselves and been expeditiously slaughtered by the natives.

It was a perfectly beautiful morning, and the wind though fair was extremly light. The skin of the sea, if I may use the expression, was as smooth as glass. We had a very deliberate view of the west side of the grand headland of Fitful Head, and an excellent opportunity of shooting dozens of porpoises as they came to the surface, with their peculiar wheel-like motion, to sun themselves

FAIR ISLE AND FOULA. 207

for a second or two. This opportunity we availed ourselves of to the extent of frightening a few of them.

We got near enough the island to see its physical features distinctly. The extreme north end rises sheer up from the sea like a wall, and on the top the grass grows to the very edge of the precipice. We see numberless incipient caves,

THE COAST.

and the process of cave-making is made very plain, layer after layer being washed off by the upward action of the water, each layer as it peels off making the arch higher.

The stacks and rocks have the most fantastic shapes. One is surmounted by a lump exactly like a lion couchant and looking over its shoulder. The sheeprock, connected with the island by a ridge not many feet above the sea level, is like a hugh sphinx with the features blurred by too much washing, and another is like an old Rhine castle in ruins.

No sooner is it plain that we are making for the shore than groups of women and children are seen on the hillocks, and almost immediately a boat is making for us, while another crew are seen rushing down to launch a second. Dividing our forces, we are rowed ashore in the two boats, and find a considerable number awaiting our arrival. The island is nearly three miles long and one and a half broad. Its highest point is about 700 feet. The population is 280—about 100 less than it was a year or two ago, but still too great. The bane of the islanders is their unwillingness to remove.

Another drawback to their prosperity is the want of a proper harbour, so as to enable them to carry on fishing on a more extensive scale. Their only fishing is along the shores for saithe. The more remunerative deep-sea fishing is, I understand, not prosecuted to any large extent.

Foula, the etymology of which is said to be Fughloe or bird island, is now our destination, lying between fifteen and twenty miles west of Shetland, and upwards of fifty from Fair Isle. It is not quite so large as Fair Isle, but is much more picturesque. Viewed from the east it presents a serrated appearance, having five large hills and two or three stacks, all leaning in the same direction like the teeth of a saw. The highest of them is about 1,400 feet.

On landing, one of our party and myself started on an expedition to the top of the Sneug Hill to see a species of gull called the bounxie or squa-gull, which is to be found only here and on Rooness Hill. This bird used to be common enough, but bird-fanciers have almost killed them out. Some years ago the proprietor of the island, Dr. Scott of Melby, began to preserve them, and they are now not so very rare.

We had scarcely started on our expedition when we were overtaken by a short wiry man, about sixty years of age, who told us that he was bound to accompany every one who landed to prevent the destruction of the bounxie. He was barefoot, and several times expressed his pity for us in climbing the hill with boots. We were rewarded for our walk by a sight of the bounxie. It is not much larger, but more compact in build, than the common gull, and grey, with speckles of white. Its flight is rapid, and its temper fierce, so much so that it is the terror of the eagle, and hence a protection to the lambs. It is certainly a very plucky bird, as we found on a nearer approach to its nest. It kept hovering close around us, and every now and then with a rapid sweep passed close to our heads. Had we gone much nearer the keeper assured us it would attack us, as it had often done him, striking him on the face with its wings. I have no doubt his account was true.

Another rare bird, the allan, is found almost exclusively on this island, and is also protected.

The rocks on the west side of Foula are particularly

P

grand, rising sheer from the sea to a height of 1,300 feet. The natives are daring fowlers, and many lives are lost in the pursuit of eggs. It is said of the Foula man, "His gutcher (grandfather) gaed before, his father gaed before, and he must expect to go over the Sneug too."

In my six visits to Shetland, I have only once failed to

THE CRADLE OF NOSS.

visit the Noup of Noss and the Orkneyman's Cave—two of the most accessible and interesting sights.

The Noup, to be seen in all its grandeur, should be approached by sea. The view from the top is very fine, but the giddy height of 600 feet can be fully appreciated only from the base of the wall-like rock. Starting, then, by boat, we pass round the south end of Bressay, where there is some grand rock scenery, in some places quite precipitous, and rising to a height of 300 or 400 feet. The action of the sea on some softer parts of the rock has cut out several large arches, through which I have passed in a boat without lowering sail. One immediately under the lighthouse is like a handsome bridge with an almost symmetrical arch. Another, called the giant's leg, also affords passage for a boat. The leg rises up from the sea like a flying buttress, as if to prop up the huge rock against which it leans, which certainly seems to need no such propping. And now we are in sight of Noss, though as yet we see only the landward grassy side of the peak.

After a tack or two we get round the end of the island, and a view that for rugged grandeur can hardly be surpassed is presented to us. Close to the island lies the Holm of Noss, a huge solid rock cut off from the island by a chasm or passage which seems, in comparison with the height, a mere fissure, but which affords a good wide berth for a boat. The Holm is quite inaccessible, except by the apparently perilous but experimentally safe enough passage by what is known as the " cradle."

The chasm is about 100 feet wide and under 200 deep. Across it, the cradle, a box large enough to contain a man and a sheep, is slung by rings on two parallel ropes, which are fastened to stakes on either side of the chasm.

This is the only mode of communication with the Holm, and it seems a dangerous one, a fall being certain death;

and yet, though it has been in use for two centuries, no life has been lost by it.

Communication with it was first suggested by the innumerable eggs with which it was seen to be covered. The offer of a cow was sufficient to tempt a fowler to scale it. The island being higher than the Holm, the ropes slope a little, and the cradle descends by its own weight. In returning, the passenger must either work his own passage, or be pulled up by his friends, no great effort being required in either case. The Holm pastures about a dozen sheep.

Steering our way between the island and the Holm, we come in full view of the Noup, which rises perpendicularly from the sea to a height of about 600 feet. Even after repeated visits it is a very grand sight; when seen for the first time it is almost overpowering. I saw it first in the month of June, and at that season the face of the rock from bottom to top was literally covered with sea-birds, and had the speckled look which a pretty heavy sprinkling of snow would produce. We fired a gun and a cloud of birds shot out, darkening the air and almost deafening us with the noise. I have a distinct recollection that on that occasion my feeling was more akin to nervousness than I have ever experienced when there was no real cause for fear. At its base there is a natural pavement of considerable breadth, the scene of many a pleasant pic-nic.

Returning by the way we came, and taking, as we pass beneath it, a last look at the airy cradle, to put a foot in which seems a tempting of Providence, we coast along Bressay, and after a not very long pull reach the cave, an opening about forty feet square at the mouth, but sixty feet in height inside. I am unable to say how far it extends inwards. I know that you can go in either so crookedly, or so far, or perhaps both, as to lose the daylight. Hence

HOMES OF THE POORER CLASS.

it is necessary to take torches with you, for without them you will neither see your way nor the beautiful stalactites which adorn the sides, some like birds, others like draped figures, and others which want similitude.

It is called the Orkneyman's Cave, from the circumstance of an Orkney sailor, when pursued by the press-gang, having taken refuge in it. Once in, he got on to a shelving rock, but did not take care to secure his boat, which drifted away, as there was a considerable ground swell. He remained a prisoner for two days, when, the sea having calmed down, he plunged in and swam to a point, from which he climbed to the top of the rock, and escaped.

The effects of a generally tempestuous sea are everywhere apparent. Near the peninsula of Northmavine is a lofty rock called the Dorholm, through which the sea has eaten a wonderful arch, 140 feet in height, and above 500 feet wide. Not far from this is another magnificent rock, called the Drenge, or Drongs, so fantastically cleft and shattered by the action of the sea as to present, from certain points of view, the appearance of a small fleet of vessels in full sail.

There is perhaps no community that gives such indications of industry among the female population as Shetland. The knitting needles and the worsted are continually in their hands, and seem to form part and parcel of the woman herself. If you take a walk towards Tingwall, you will meet or pass dozens of women going for or returning with peats from the hill, all busy knitting—one a stocking, another a stout shawl or cravat. The finer articles—scarfs, veils, and lace shawls, which are often exquisitely fine—cannot be worked in this off-hand way, and are reserved for leisure hours at home.

The poorer classes generally wear, not shoes, but "rivlins"—a kind of sandal made of untanned cow-hide, or sometimes sealskin, with the hair outside, and lashed to the foot with thongs.

All the wool of the pure Shetland sheep is fine, but the finest grows under the neck, and is never shorn off, but "rooed," that is, gently pulled. It is said that an ounce of wool can by skill be spun into upwards of 1,000 yards of three-ply thread. Stockings can be

knitted of such fineness as to be easily drawn through a finger-ring.

To Shetlanders the sea and its products are of paramount importance, and some account of their fisheries is accordingly indispensable.

The boat used is the Norway yawl, fitted either for sailing or rowing, and with six of a crew. Each boat has between seven and eight miles of line and 1,000 hooks. The lines are set in the evening, and if the first haul is not successful they may bait and set them again. They sometimes remain out two nights, if the weather is fine, during which they must content themselves with very little sleep and scanty fare. They generally take nothing with them but oat-cakes and water.

The ha'af fishing has many a sad tale to tell of drowning and disaster. Their boats of eighteen feet keel and six feet beam are little fitted to weather a severe storm. Anxious not to lose their lines—in many cases their all—the poor fishers bravely try to keep their ground, and often lose their lives as well. Such calamities are more overwhelming, from the fact that the crew of a boat are often all members of the same family. At such terrible times the warmth and kindliness of the Shetland character come out admirably, one family bringing up one orphan, another another, doubtless from the feeling that next season, or next week, their own little ones may be in similar case.

Hibbert, in his "History of Shetland," mentions a toast that used to be, and perhaps is still, given at a rude festival about the beginning of the ha'af fishing:—" Men an' brethren, lat wis (us) raise a helt (health). Here's first to da glory o' God, an' da guid o' wir (our) ain puir sauls, wir wordy landmaister, an' wir lovin' meatmither; helt to man, death to fish, an' guid growth i' da grund." When this fishing, is over, and they are about to return to their harvest, the toast is, " God open the mouth o' da gray fish (sillocks), an' haud His hand aboot da corn."

ARCTIC SEAS.

ARCTIC SEAS.

CHAPTER I.

SEARCH FOR FRANKLIN.

WHETHER or not it were right for Government to despatch the expedition of 1845, it was undoubtedly right, when that expedition was felt to be in peril of destruction, that every effort should be made to rescue the brave men of whom it was composed.

And nobly was the duty fulfilled. From 1848, when fears first began to be entertained for the safety of Franklin's crews, seventeen different attempts have been made to save them, and, when rescue seemed all but hopeless, to ascertain at least their fate.

The melancholy knowledge has at last been gained, and we propose briefly to repeat the story, than which we know none more touching in the history of modern adventure.

On the 26th of May, 1845, Sir John Franklin sailed from England in command of her Majesty's ships the *Erebus* and *Terror*, already well tried in the expedition to the Antarctic Ocean under Sir James Ross. He was accompanied by Captain Crozier, whose experience in the Arctic Seas had been gained under Parry and Ross, and by a picked body of officers and men, numbering in all 134 persons.

His orders were to endeavour to force his way through Lancaster Sound and Barrow's Strait to the longitude of Cape Walker, and thence to seek a passage to Behring Strait in a southerly direction; or, in the event of the ice not permitting him to adopt this route, to explore the great opening to the north, called Wellington Channel, and endeavour to pierce westward in a higher latitude. The naval service had none better fitted for so responsible and arduous a post.

The courage and the nerve of Franklin had been tried in the actions of Copenhagen and Trafalgar. His integrity and fitness for command, besides the power of gaining the affections of all with whom he came in contact, had been displayed in his administration under circumstances of no ordinary difficulty of the governorship of Tasmania. In former days he had earned from the sailors for his vessel the title of Franklin's Paradise. Already, too, he had, on three different occasions, conducted—once as second in command, once in conjunction with Sir John Richardson, and once as leader—expeditions to the Arctic Sea and to the northern shores of America. In these he had acquired a reputation for daring and endurance, tempered with a sagacity and consideration for the lives of those under his charge, which made his name even then a household word in the service.

No one who has read the thrilling history of his retreat on the second of these expeditions, across the wastes which extend to the east of the Coppermine River, can doubt that, in this new field, every effort of which humanity is capable would be made to win the goal, and when that was no longer possible, to save the remnants of his crew.

And, above all, he was a sincere and earnest Christian. " He had a cheerful buoyancy of mind, which, sustained by religious principles of a depth known only to his most intimate friends, was not depressed in the most gloomy times." So writes Richardson, who knew him well, and who, " during upwards of twenty-five years, had his entire confidence, and in times of great difficulty and distress, when all conventional disguise was out of the question, beheld his calmness and unaffected piety."

With such a leader, the prospect of success seemed doubly bright, and officers and men were alike sanguine of a speedy and triumphant issue. The letters received from them from the coast of Greenland spoke in the warmest language of their admiration of their commander, and their happiness in serving under him. And Franklin's own last utterance, as he sailed away into the night which, for him and them, was never more to know a dawn, was one of strong reliance on the hand of Him whom he had served through life, and by whom, we may feel well assured, though no word has come forth from his icy grave to tell us, he was not forsaken in his time of need.

"Again," he writes to Parry, in, we believe, the last

WHALERS IN BAFFIN'S BAY.

letter received from the expedition, and just a fortnight before it was seen for the last time. "Again, my dear Parry, I will recommend my dearest wife and daughter to your kind regards; I know that they will heartily join with many dear friends in fervent prayer that the almighty Power may guide and protect us, and that the blessing of his Holy Spirit may rest upon us. Our prayers, I trust, will be offered up with equal fervour for those inestimable blessings to be vouchsafed to them, and to all who love the Lord Jesus in sincerity and truth. I humbly pray that God's best blessing may attend yourself, Lady Parry, and your family."

The vessels were seen by a whaler in Baffin's Bay on the 26th of June, 1845, waiting for an opening in the ice to permit them to enter Lancaster Sound. They were never seen again.

In 1847, public anxiety began to be shown for the safety of the explorers, and in the following year two expeditions were despatched in search; the one, consisting of two vessels, to Behring Strait; the other, under the command of Sir John Richardson, overland, to the north-eastern shores of America, which in that and the following year were traced from the extreme west to the estuary of the Coppermine.

In 1849, Sir James Ross, also with two vessels, examined the shores of Barrow's Strait, and in a sledge excursion, traced the western coast of North Somerset to the latitude of 72° 38', or within a short distance of the spot where, as we shall see, Captain M'Clintock wintered on his last voyage, and in the direct track, as it has since proved, of the missing ships. But next year on leaving his winter quarters, he was surrounded by the drift-ice, and carried helplessly eastward through the whole length of Lancaster Sound, into Davis' Strait, where he was only released at a period of the year too late to allow of the resumption of the search.

Meanwhile, however, the work was being vigorously pursued by other hands; and in 1850 no less than five distinct expeditions started from England, and two vessels, fitted out by the munificence of Mr. Grinnell, an American merchant, from New York. Into the details of these several explorations we need not enter; but two of them, of which the Grinnell expedition was one, divide the merit of having discovered the first traces of the missing ships.

These were found in Beechey Island, at the mouth of Wellington Channel, where it was discovered that Franklin had spent the winter of 1845-6, and where the tombs of three of his men, who had died early in the latter year, remained. Curiously enough, not one record or indication of any kind was found to point to the route which had been subsequently pursued by them; but it was augured by many that they would follow a northern course through Wellington Channel, and should be sought for on the shores of the great Polar Ocean, indicated by Penny and by Kane.

In this dubiety as to their after course, the search went on in various directions. Kane, in command of the *Advance*, fitted out by the renewed liberality of Mr. Grinnell, made that wonderful voyage to Smith's Strait, which stands without an equal even in these stirring annals; Kennedy, accompanied by Lieutenant Bellot of the French navy, who fell a martyr to his devotion in the

WINTER IN WELLINGTON CHANNEL.

cause of humanity, all but touched the spot where, as we now know, the abandoned vessels were lying in the ice; Collinson and M'Clure forced their way along the northern coasts of America, the one to complete in safety the longest voyage ever known in the Arctic seas, the other—after two winters spent in the ice, and at last abandoning the vessel in despair—to effect, on foot, the escape of himself and his crew to another of the ships engaged in the search, and win the proud distinction of being the first to pass from west to east across these dreary wastes.

Many other attempts were also made, fifteen vessels in all being engaged in the search between 1850 and 1853, but all in vain. The stanchion of a ship's ice-plank, picked up by Dr. Rae, and the fragment of an iron bolt and of a hutch frame, seen by Captain Collinson in the possession of the Eskimos, were the only indications that could be connected with Franklin, and even these were susceptible of other explanations.

But in 1854 the veil was lifted at last, and the traces of a terrible tragedy dimly disclosed to the startled seekers. In that year Dr. Rae, who, with indefatigable perseverance, had returned a third time to the search in the vicinity of King William's Land, encountered, in the course of his explorations between Pelly and Inglis Bays, a party of Eskimos, in whose possession were found a great variety of articles, and many pieces of silver plate, known to have belonged to officers both of the *Erebus* and *Terror*.

From these natives he learned that another party the same tribe had met, in the spring of 1850, a band about forty white men dragging a boat and sledges alc the coast side of King William's Land, and maki apparently for the Great Fish River. None of th could speak the Eskimo language; but, from their sig the natives understood that their vessels had b(

DRAGGING BOAT ACROSS ICE-FIELDS.

crushed in the ice, and that they were then proceed where they hoped to find deer to shoot. They] purchased a small seal from the natives, and from thin appearance of the men—all of whom, with exception of one, who appeared to be an officer, w dragging on the haul-ropes of the sledge—were thou to be running short of provisions.

At a later period of the same year, the corpses of some thirty persons, as well as some graves, were found by the Eskimos on the mainland, and five dead bodies on an island close by—points agreeing in description with Montreal Island and Point Ogle, at the mouth of the river above referred to. Some of the unfortunate band must have survived even as late as May or June, (or until the return of the wild fowl,) as shots had been heard about that time, and fresh bones and feathers gathered in the immediate vicinity.

The melancholy news was verified by the articles received; but the moment it was learned, an anxious desire was felt to explore the spot where the last moments of the ill-fated crews had been spent, and which Dr. Rae, from the failure of his provisions and the state of the health of his party, had been unable to accomplish. Mr. Anderson, one of their chief factors, was accordingly despatched by the Hudson Bay Company, in 1855, down the Great Fish River, to visit the scene of the catastrophe, and endeavour to procure additional information from a careful search for any records that might have been deposited, as well as from the tribes in the vicinity.

Unfortunately, this journey had a very imperfect result. The expedition was poorly supplied with the means of extending its operations. No interpreter could be procured, and all communication with the tribes had to be carried on by signs.

Numerous traces were indeed discovered of the missing

crews, and a number of additional articles purchased from the Eskimos, but not a scrap of paper or record of any kind. The absence, too, of any graves, or cairns, or human bones, led many to the inference that the actual spot referred to by the natives, in their communication with Rae, had not yet been reached.

Under these circumstances, an earnest appeal was made to Lord Palmerston, in June, 1856, by a number of men of science, and others who had taken a deep interest in Arctic discovery, and repeated, in an admirable letter addressed to him by Lady Franklin, in the December of the same year, to despatch a final expedition to the narrow and circumscribed area now known as that within which the missing vessels or their remains must lie, and the access to which appeared to be free from many of the difficulties and dangers which had hitherto attended the search. The Prime Minister, it is understood, had personally every desire to carry out the wishes of his memorialists, but was precluded from acceding to their petition.

Lady Franklin, however, had resolved that, if the Government declined, she should herself exhaust her fortune in this last effort; and, aided by the contributions of many tried friends, she purchased the little screw yacht, the *Fox*, of 177 tons, and placed her, in April 1857, under the command of Captain M'Clintock, who had earned a distinguished name in the Arctic Seas, under Sir James Ross and Austin and Kellett.

The refitting of the vessel was pressed forward with

the utmost speed at Aberdeen by her original builders, and a small body of twenty-five men, seventeen of whom had previously served in the search, carefully selected for her crew. The difficulty, indeed, was to know whom to prefer from the number of volunteers who came forward.

"Expeditions of this kind," says M‘Clintock, "are always popular with seamen, and innumerable were the applications made to me; but still more abundant were the offers 'to serve in any capacity,' which poured in from all parts of the country, from people of all classes, many of whom had never seen the sea. It was of course impossible to accede to any of these latter proposals; yet, for my own part, I could not but feel gratified at such convincing proofs that the spirit of the country was favourable to us, and that the ardent love of hardy enterprise still lives among Englishmen as of old, to be cherished, I trust, as the most valuable of our national characteristics—as that which has so largely contributed to make England what she is."

The Government, though declining to send out an expedition themselves, liberally contributed to the provisioning of the vessel.

By the end of June, the preparations were complete; and on the 30th, Lady Franklin, accompanied by her niece, visited the vessel to bid farewell. The same evening the vessel set sail.

ARCTIC SEAS.

CHAPTER II.

SEARCH FOR FRANKLIN.

ON the 12th July, the *Fox* was off Cape Farewell, the southernmost part of Greenland, and on the 24th reached the Danish settlement of Godhaab, on the east coast of Davis' Strait, and transferred one of the crew, who had shown symptoms of diseased lungs, to a vessel about to leave for Copenhagen.

At Disco Bay, they secured the services of a young Eskimo as dog-driver, and a team of dogs, afterwards supplemented at the settlements of Proven and Upernavick, still farther to the north. On the 6th August, they arrived at the latter cluster of huts, well known to the readers of Kane's second voyage as the first inhabited spot he reached in his memorable escape from Smith's Strait in 1855.

They had on board, as interpreter, Petersen, one of the party who accompanied Kane on that expedition, whose enthusiasm in the cause had led him to join M'Clintock from Copenhagen, just before the yacht left Aberdeen, though he had only returned six days previously from Greenland, after a year's absence from his family. Here the last letters for home were landed, and the vessel's head turned seaward.

The drifting ice, which invariably obstructs the passage to Baffin's Bay, was reached next day; and after an attempt to find a middle passage, in the course of which they were once caught in the margin of the floe, and only escaped by the assistance of the screw, it was resolved to look for an opening on the north. On the 12th, they reached Melville Bay, in lat. 79°, but found the whole sea to the northward blocked up by the ice.

It was too late in the year to retrace their steps with a reasonable hope of reaching Barrow's Strait before the season closed; and in the hope of the autumnal winds drifting southwards the pack, and so opening up a passage, they anchored to a berg, and, after three days' calm, were gladdened by their anticipations being realised, and finding themselves steaming along a widening lane of water through the ice to the north-west. But on the following evening the pack closed in around them, and they were cut off from all power either of advancing or retreating.

The drift next day continued to the north-west, and carried the little vessel, of course, along with it; but on the 20th it ceased, and M'Clintock already began to apprehend the possibility of having to winter in the pack. It was a trying thought; but he could only abide his fate, and resolve, if it was to be such as he feared, " to repeat the trial next year, and in the end, with God's aid, perform his sacred duty."

It was clear, at last, that there was to be no escape till spring, and the preparations for wintering were forthwith begun. They faced the gloomy prospect of more than half a year of absolute inutility with cheerful resignation; and the disappointment which the delay would entail on the highly-wrought expectations of Lady Franklin, appears to have caused more regret than any mere selfish anticipations as to themselves.

A school was opened on board by Dr. Walker, the surgeon and naturalist of the expedition, and the spirit of inquiry shown by his pupils is spoken of by M'Clintock as gratifying in the extreme. This, with the exercising the men in the construction of snow huts, as preparative for their spring travelling, and the hunting the seal and bear, did much to while away the monotonous days of their imprisonment. On the 1st of November, they bade farewell to the sun; on the 30th, the thermometer had descended to 64° below freezing.

On the 4th December, the first death took place on board—the engine-driver having fallen down a hatchway, and received such injuries that he died two days afterwards.

And now, too, a steady drift from the north set in,

POLAR BEARS.

and, day by day, they became aware that, in their icy prison, they were driving farther and farther from their destination. In the course of December, they had been carried southward sixty-seven miles.

The month of April was full of days of anxiety and excitement. Gales from the north told severely on the continuity of the ice; and on one occasion a rift was escaped with difficulty. At last, on the 17th, the ship was fairly adrift, and, in a heaving gale, running fast along the narrow channels that opened up to the south and east; but only to be again frozen up on the following day.

A week later, and the great swell of the Atlantic was felt for the first time, " lifting its crest five feet above the hollow of the sea, causing its thick covering of icy fragments to dash against each other" and the little bark. "The pack had taken upon itself," as Dr Kane had expressed it, "the functions of an ocean," and, amidst a chaos of contending masses and shattered bergs, they had to steer their course to the open sea.

Knowing well that near the edge of the pack the sea would be very heavy and dangerous, he had yet taken advantage of a favourable wind to run what he well calls his ice-tournament, and make an effort for escape. A few hours after the wind failed, and the vessel had to trust to her steam-power alone. By this time the swell of the ocean, covered with countless masses of ice and numerous large berg-pieces, to touch one of which latter must have been instant destruction, was rising ten feet above the trough of the sea. The shocks became alarmingly heavy; it was necessary to steer head on to the swell, which was sufficient to send the waves in showers of spray over an iceberg sixty feet high, as they slowly passed alongside.

THE EDGE OF A PACK.

Gradually, as the day wore on, the swell increased into a sea; but still, as by magic, they escaped all contact with any but the young ice, and, by the afternoon, found the latter become more loose, and clear spaces of water visible ahead. They steered on at greater speed—received fewer, though still more severe, shocks—had room at length to steer clear of the heavier pieces—and at last, at 8 p.m. on the 25th, "emerged from the villanous pack, and were running fast through straggling pieces into a clear sea. The engines were stopped, and Mr. Brand (the engineer, and the only one since the death of Scott able to work them) permitted to rest, after eighteen hours' duty."

"Throughout the day," says M'Clintock, "I trembled for the safety of the rudder and screw. Deprived of the one or the other, even for half an hour, I think our fate would have been sealed. . . . On many occasions the engines were stopped dead by ice checking the screw; once it was some minutes before it could be got to revolve again. Anxious moments those! After yesterday's experience, I can understand how men's hair has grown grey in a few hours. Had self-reliance been my only support and hope, it is not impossible that I might have illustrated the fact. Under the circumstances, I did my best to ensure our safety, looked as stoical as possible, and inwardly trusted that God would favour our exertions.

"What a relief ours has been, not only from eight months' imprisonment, but from the perils of that one day! Had our little vessel been destroyed after the ice broke up, there remained no hope for us. But we have been brought safely through, and are all truly grateful, I hope and believe."

During the 242 days in which they had been embedded in the ice, they had been carried southwards no less than 1,385 miles.

They now steered for Holsteinborg, a port of Greenland; and, after a short stay to take in provisions, began again to coast southwards to their old quarters in Melville Bay, which, after more than one hard battle with the ice, and a narrow escape of leaving their vessel on a reef of rocks near Buchan Island, on which she ran aground, they reached on the 19th June, two months earlier than in the previous year. The passage across Baffin's Bay to the mouth of Lancaster Sound was still one of extreme difficulty, in the course of which the imprisonment of last year seemed more than once likely to be their fate again; but, on the 16th July, they were fairly over, and "dodging about in a tub of water" off Cape Warrender.

The ice still blocked up the whole of Lancaster Sound, and three weeks were devoted to a visit to Pond's Bay, some seventy miles farther north, and to a close interrogation of the Eskimo tribes in the vicinity, as to some rumours of wrecks reported to have taken place in their neighbourhood, but which it was ascertained were unfounded. On the 9th of August, they were again off Lancaster Sound, now comparatively open; and, two days later, anchored off Beechey Island, where, as already mentioned, Franklin spent his first winter.

On the 16th, the *Fox* sailed from Beechey Island for Peel Channel, by which it was hoped that an access

SUMMER IN LANCASTER SOUND.

might be gained to Victoria Strait, on the shores of which the expected traces of the *Erebus* and *Terror* were to be sought.

For two days this route was pursued without interruption; but on the evening of the second, the disappointed crew beheld in their front a sheet of unbroken ice, extending from shore to shore. Not daring to lose a moment in what would most probably have been a fruitless attempt to force a passage, the vessel's head was again turned, and the last chance of an access by the parallel estuary of Prince Regent's Inlet and Bellot's Strait, reported to form a passage to the open water on the west, tried by their now doubly-anxious commander.

The crisis of the voyage was fast approaching. "Does Bellot Strait really exist? If so, is it free from ice?"

They reached its mouth on the 20th, and found locked ice streaming out of the opening. The next day they had forced their way half through, but the lock to the west was so consolidated, that though seventeen days were spent in repeated efforts, and they were at last enabled on the 6th September to steer right through the passage, all further progress was at last abandoned as hopeless, and the yacht, on the 28th, made secure for the second winter in a little creek on the northern shore.

"To-day we are unbending sails and laying up the engines; uncertainty no longer exists, here we are compelled to remain; and if we have not been so successful in our voyaging as a month ago we had good reason to expect, we may still hope that Fortune will smile upon our more humble, yet more arduous, pedestrian explorations—'Hope on, hope ever!'"

We hurry over the details of the winter months, the monotonous and dreary solitude of which was endured with a cheerfulness which speaks volumes for the crew and their officers; and look in again upon the little band as on the 17th of February, 1859, the sledge parties left the ship for the first time on their several journeys.

From the western extremity of Bellot's Strait, the coast of Boothia, and the whole coast of King William's Island, to the mouth of the Great Fish River, was to be thoroughly explored; while to the north, the coast of Prince of Wales' Island was to be traced to the point in latitude 72° 50′, reached by Sherard Osborn in 1851.

Captain Young, of the mercantile marine, whose enthusiasm in the cause had not only induced him to abandon lucrative appointments in command, and accept of a subordinate post on board the *Fox*, but to subscribe £500 in aid of her outfit, was now, with a few men, about to start for the purpose of depositing provisions in the last-mentioned direction, in view of the more extended search in the spring, and Captain M'Clintock, with Peterson and another, to leave for the south, for a similar purpose, and to communicate with the Eskimos of Boothia. Both parties returned in safety in the following month, and M'Clintock with important intelligence, bearing on the main object of the expedition.

He had encountered, in the immediate vicinity of the

magnetic pole, in latitude 70°, a small band of natives one of whom had on his dress *a naval button*.

"It came," they said, "from some white men who were starved upon an island where there are salmon

AN ESKIMO VILLAGE.

(that is, in a river), and that the iron of which their knives were made came from the same place. One of these men said he had been to the island to obtain wood and iron, but none of them had seen the white men."

"Next morning, the entire village population arrived, amounting to about forty-five souls, from aged people to infants in arms, and bartering commenced very briskly. First of all we purchased all the relics of the lost expedition, consisting of six silver spoons and forks, a silver medal, the property of Mr. A. M'Donald, assistant-surgeon, part of a gold chain, several buttons, and knives made of the iron and wood of the wreck, also bows and arrows constructed of materials obtained from the same source.

"None of these people had seen the whites; one man said he had seen their bones upon the island where they died, but some were buried. Petersen also understood him to say that the boat was crushed by the ice. Almost all of them had part of the plunder.

"Next morning, 4th March, several natives came to us again. I bought a spear six and a half feet long from a man who told Petersen distinctly that a ship having three masts had been crushed by the ice out in the sea to the west of King William's Island, but that all the people landed safely; he was not one of those who were eye-witnesses of it; the ship sunk, so nothing was obtained by the natives from her; all that they have got, he said, came from the island in the river."

M'Clintock, on receiving this intelligence, hurried back to the *Fox* with all the speed in his power, and organised plans for a careful and deliberate search of the district in question. He had encountered great hardships on this rapid journey, during which he had travelled, in twenty-five days, 420 miles, in a temperature the mean of which was 62° below freezing.

On the 2nd of April all was ready for the start. Lieutenant Hobson, the second in command, was entrusted with the examination of the western coast of King William's Island, M'Clintock following the bend of Boothia to the east, exploring the eastern shore of the island, and, after a visit to Montreal Island, returning in the track of Hobson. The two parties proceeded in company to the spot where the natives had been met with, and gained from them, on this second visit, additional information.

"The young man who sold the knife told us that the body of a man was found on board the ship; that he must have been a very large man, and had long teeth; this is all he recollected having been told, for he was quite a child at the time.

"They both told us it was in the fall of the year—that is, August or September—when the ships were destroyed; that all the white people went away to the 'large river,' taking a boat or boats with them, and that in the following winter their bones were found there."

ARCTIC SEAS.

CHAPTER III.

SEARCH FOR FRANKLIN.

AT Cape Victoria, Hobson and M'Clintock parted company, and we now follow the steps of the latter. Crossing over the channel which separates Boothia from King William's Island, he passed several deserted villages of the Eskimos, around which numerous chips and shavings of wood from the last expedition were seen, and at last reached a cluster of thirty or forty inhabited huts, where he purchased for a few needles six spoons and forks with the crests or initials of Franklin, Crozier, and others of their companions, and was told that it was five days' journey across the island to the scene of the wreck, of which but little now remained.

The site of the wreck lying exactly in Hobson's track, in which he was himself to return, M'Clintock continued his journey to the southern extremity of the island, and thereafter crossed over to Point Ogle and Montreal Island, at the foot of the Great Fish River. A careful examination of the latter, the last spot in which the survivors of the last party had been seen by the natives, yielded nothing to the seekers but a piece of a preserved meat tin and some scraps of copper and iron hoops; and with much disappointment they again turned northwards on the 19th of May.

Five days afterwards they recrossed to King William's Island, and followed the windings of the western shore. Here, on the 25th, "while slowly walking along on a gravel ridge near the beach, which the winds kept partially bare of snow," in all the solemn stillness of an Arctic midnight, they came upon a human skeleton stretched upon its face, with scraps of clothing lying round, and appearing through the snow. The victim appeared to have been a young man, slight build, and, from his dress, a steward or officer's servant. A pocket-book found close by afforded hopes of his identification, but though every effort was made to decipher the hard frozen leaves, nothing but a few detached sentences, in no way bearing on the fate of the expedition, has been made out.

"It was a melancholy truth that the old woman spoke when she said, 'they fell down, and died as they walked along.' . . . . This poor man seems to have selected the bare ridge top, as affording the least tiresome walking, and to have fallen upon his face in the position in which we found him."

They now approached a large cairn, originally built by Simpson in 1839, and where, as it must have been passed by the last crews, they eagerly anticipated finding some record; but a careful search proved wholly fruitless, and from the appearance of the cairn, they were led to believe that it had already been examined and rifled by the Eskimos. Twelve miles further, however, they came upon a cairn built by Hobson's party, who had reached the same point a few days before, and in which was deposited a note, announcing the discovery of the record so ardently sought, under a third cairn, still further to the south, and on the site of one formerly built by Sir James Ross.

"There is an error in this document," says Captain M'Clintock; "namely, that the *Erebus* and *Terror* wintered at Beechey Island in 1846-7; the correct dates should have been 1845-6. A glance at the date at the top and bottom of the record proves this, but in all other respects the tale is told in as few words as possible of their wonderful success up to that date, May, 1847. . . . .

"Seldom has such an amount of success been accorded to an Arctic navigator in a single season, and when the *Erebus* and *Terror* were secured at Beechey Island for the coming winter of 1845-6, the results of their first year's labour must have been most cheering. These results were the exploration of Wellington and Queen's Channel, and the addition to our charts of the extensive lands on either hand. In 1846 they proceeded to the

DISCOVERY AT THE ROSS-CAIRN.

south-west, and eventually reached within twelve miles of the north extreme of King William's Land, when their progress was arrested by the approaching winter of 1846-7. That winter appears to have passed without any serious loss of life; and when in the spring Lieutenant Gore leaves with a party for some especial purpose, and very probably to connect the unknown coast-line of King William's Land between Point Victory and Cape Herschel, those on board the *Erebus* and *Terror* were 'all well,' and the gallant Franklin still commanded."

But, alas! round the margin of the paper upon which Lieutenant Gore, in 1847, wrote those words of hope and promise, a sad and touching postscript had been added by another hand on the 28th April in the following year.

"There is some additional marginal information relative to the transfer of the document to its present position (viz., the site of Sir James Ross's pillar) from a spot four miles to the northward, near Point Victory, where it had been originally deposited by the *late* Commander Gore. This little word *late* shows us that he too, within the twelvemonth, had passed away.

"In the short space of twelve months how mournful had become the history of Franklin's expedition, how changed from the cheerful 'all well' of Graham Gore! The spring of 1847 found them within 90 miles of the known sea off the coast of America; and to men who had already, in two seasons, sailed over 500 miles of previously unexplored waters, how confident must they then have felt that that forthcoming navigable season of 1847 would see their ships pass over so short an intervening space! It was ruled otherwise. Within a month after Lieutenant Gore placed the record on Point Victory, the much-loved leader of the expedition, Sir John Franklin, was dead; and the following spring found Captain Crozier, upon whom the command had devolved, at King William's Land, endeavouring to save his starving men, 105 souls in all, from a terrible death, by retreating to the Hudson Bay territories up the Back or Great Fish River.

"A sad tale was never told in fewer words. There is something deeply touching in their extreme simplicity, and they show in the strongest manner that both the leaders of this retreating party were actuated by the loftiest sense of duty, and met with calmness and decision the fearful alternative of a last bold struggle for life, rather than perish without effort on board their ships; for we well know that the *Erebus* and *Terror* were only provisioned up to July, 1848. . . . .

"Lieutenant Hobson's note told me that he found quantities of clothing and articles of all kinds lying about the cairn, as if these men, aware that they were retreating for their lives, had there abandoned everything which they considered superfluous."

But there was yet a third, and not the least affecting, discovery to be made by the returning band. As they reached the western extremity of the island, they came in sight of a wide and desolate bay, on the southern shore of which was found a large boat, mounted on a sledge; "another melancholy relic which Hobson had found and examined a few days before, as his note left here informed me, but he had failed to discover record, journal, pocket-book, or memorandum of any description."

In the boat was that which transfixed the searchers with awe: the portions of two skeletons—the one of a slight young person; the other of a large, strongly-made, middle-aged man. Near the former, which lay in the bow of the boat, was found the fragment of a pair of worked slippers, and beside them a pair of small strong shooting half-boots.

"The other skeleton was in a somewhat more perfect state, and was enveloped with clothes and furs; it lay across the boat, under the after-thwart. Close beside it were found five watches; and there were two double-barrelled guns—*one barrel in each loaded and cocked*—standing muzzle upwards against the boat's side. It may be imagined with what deep interest these sad relics were scrutinised, and how anxiously every fragment of clothing was turned over in search of pockets and pocket-books, journals, or even names. Five or six small books were found, all of them scriptural or devotional works, except the 'Vicar of Wakefield.' One little book, 'Christian Melodies,' bore an inscription upon the title-page from the donor to G. G. (Graham Gore?) A small Bible contained numerous marginal notes, and whole passages underlined. Besides these books, the covers of a New Testament and Prayer-book were found. . . . .

"The only provisions we could find were tea and chocolate; of the former very little remained, but there were nearly forty pounds of the latter. These articles alone could never support life in such a climate, and we found neither biscuit nor meat of any kind. . . . .

"I was astonished to find that the sledge was directed to the N.E., exactly for the next point of land for which we ourselves were travelling!

"A little reflection led me to satisfy my own mind at least, that the boat was returning to the ships; and in no other way can I account for two men having been left in her, than by supposing the party were unable to drag the boat further, and that these two men, not being able to keep pace with their shipmates, were therefore left by them supplied with such provisions as could be spared, to last until the return of the others from the ship with a fresh stock.

"The same reasons which may be assigned for the return of this detachment from the main body, will also serve to account for their not having come back to their boat. In both instances they appear to have greatly overrated their strength, and the distance they could travel in a given time."

What thoughts must those have been of that lonely pair in the deserted boat, as hour by hour they gazed across the dreary wastes for the comrades who never returned, or of that strong man in his solitary death-watch when his sole companion had sunk beside him into his eternal sleep!

Neither by Hobson nor M'Clintock had any trace been found of the missing vessels, and at last the latter reached the cairn where the record above referred to had been

ARCTIC BIRDS.

discovered by his lieutenant. Around it were found an immense variety of relics—stores, pick-axes, shovels, compasses, medicine-chest, &c., and a heap of clothing four feet high—but not one scrap of writing.

From this point the coast was carefully explored to the

south, but no further traces were found, and on the 19th June the weary searchers reached once more "their poor dear lovely little *Fox*."

Little is said by M'Clintock of the determination or endurance required bearing on so extended and minute a search on an Arctic shore for a period of more than two months and a-half. The temperature was frequently nearly 30° below zero, with cutting north winds, bright sun, and intense severe glare. The men had each to drag a weight of 200 lbs., to encamp every evening in snow huts, which it cost something like two hours of hard labour, at the close of a long day's walk, to build, and in which the very blankets and clothes became loaded with ice.

"When our low doorway was carefully blocked up with snow, and the cooking lamp alight, the temperature quickly rose, so that the walls became glazed and our bedding thawed; but the cooking over, as the doorway partially opened, it as quickly fell again, so that it was impossible to sleep, or even to hold one's pannikin of tea without putting our mitts on, so intense was the cold."

Under these privations, Hobson at last had fairly broken down, and for many days before he reached the yacht had been totally unable to walk or even stand without assistance. He was obliged in consequence to be dragged home in one of the sledges, but by the time M'Clintock arrived had already begun to mend. One death had taken place during their absence, making, with that of the engineer, who had suddenly died of apoplexy during the winter, the third that had occurred in the voyage.

Captain Young had been compelled to return some time before from his explorations to the north for medical assistance, his health having been greatly injured by exposure and fatigue; but after having recruited, had started again to renew the search, in the face of a strong written protest by the doctor; and his continued absence was now the only cause of anxiety to the little band. At last M'Clintock, with five men, set off to seek him, and two days after, to his great joy, encountered him on his return, so weakened that he too was travelling in the dog-sledge, but with the particulars of a long and most interesting exploration of new ground, though without any traces of the missing crews.

Every part of the proposed search had now been fully and efficiently performed, and all thoughts were busied towards home. By the middle of July, they were ready to start; but it was not until the 10th of the following month, and after many anxious hours, that the little vessel was fairly under way.

Their passage homewards was almost without interruption from the ice, except for four days, when, though it closed them in, its friendly shelter apparently saved them from the worse fate of being driven ashore in a heavy gale off Creswell Bay. Without either engineer or engine-driver, M'Clintock had himself to superintend the working of the engines, and found, at first, the unwonted task not a little arduous, not only from its novelty, but the continuous attention required, extending, on one occasion, to twenty-four hours' incessant work. On the 21st, they gained the open sea, and, eight days later, were lying in the quiet security of Godhaven, reading their first letters from home, after a lapse of two years; and, on the 20th September, arrived in safety in the Irish Channel.

"I will not," writes the commander, in the simple and manly phrase which lends to his volume such an additional charm, "intrude upon the reader, who has followed me through the pages of this simple narrative, any description of my feelings on finding the enthusiasm with which we were all received on landing upon our native shores. The blessing of Providence had attended our efforts, and more than a full measure of approval from our friends and countrymen has been our reward. For myself, the testimonial given me by the officers and crew of the *Fox* has touched me perhaps more than all. The purchase of a gold chronometer, for presentation to me, was the first use the men made of their earnings; and as long as I live, it will remind me of that perfect harmony, that mutual esteem and good-will, which made our ship's company a happy little community, and contributed materially to the success of the expedition."

NORWAY.

NORWAY.

CHAPTER I.

THE LAND.

Do you wish your lungs to expand, your eyes to dilate, your muscles to spring, and your spirits to leap?—then come to Norway! I repeat it—be you man or woman, grave or gay; if you ever indulge in lofty aspirations, in bold contemplations, in desperate imaginings—come to Norway, and you will receive much satisfaction, I assure you.

Are you a man? You will find subject and occasion for your manhood. Are you a woman? You will find yourself at the fountain-head of the sublime and beautiful. Are you scientific? The rocks are bold and bare—the flora rich and varied. Birds and beasts of many kinds there are; glaciers, too, miles and miles of them, filling up the valleys, and covering the mountain tops—awaiting the inspection of your critical eye. Are you a painter? There is ample field for the wildest pencil and the boldest brush.

Are you a fisher? Here is your terrestrial paradise. But you must be a fisher of the rough school, not "a follower of the gentle art." Can you wade all day in snow-water? Can you swim down a roaring rapid—perchance shoot over a cataract, and count it but a trifle—with a twenty foot rod in your hands, and a thirty-pound salmon at the end of your line, making for the sea at the rate of twenty miles an hour? Then, by all means come to Norway. But you must be possessed of a singularly patient and self-denying character. Mark that well.

Are you a daring mountaineer? The mountains of Gamle Norge (Old Norway), though not so high as those of the Himalaya range, are high enough for most men. The eagle will guide you to heights—if you can follow him—on which human foot has never rested.

Do you love the sunshine? Think of the great luminary that rules the day, rolling through the bright blue sky all the twenty-four hours round. There is no night here in summer, but a long, bright, beautiful day, as if Nature were rejoicing in the banishment of night from earth for ever.

But, above all, do you love simplicity, urbanity, unsophisticated kindness in man? Are you a student of human nature, and fond of dwelling on its brighter aspects? Then once more I say, come to Norway, for you will find her sons and daughters overflowing with the milk of human kindness.

THE LAND.

I was fortunate enough to come to Norway in a friend's yacht, and voyaged along the west coast from south to north.

It is impossible to give any one an adequate idea of what is meant by sailing among the islands off the coast of Norway, or of the delights attendant on such navigation. If you would understand this thoroughly, you must experience it for yourself. Here is a brief summary of pleasures.

Yachting without sea-sickness. Scenery ever changing, always beautiful and wild beyond description. Landing possible, desirable, frequent. Expectation ever on tiptoe. Hope constant. Agreeable surprises perpetual. Tremendous astonishments numerous, and variety without end. Could any one desire more?

The islands extend along the whole coast in myriads. I presume that their actual number never has been, and never can be, ascertained. Some are so huge that you mistake them for the mainland. Others are so small that you might take them for castles floating on the sea. And on many of them—most of them, perhaps—you find small houses—quaint, gable-ended, wooden, and red-tile-roofed—in the midst of small patches of verdure, or, not unfrequently, perched upon the naked rock.

In some cases a small cottage may be seen unrelieved by any blade of green, sticking in a crevice of the rock like some miniature Noah's Ark, that had taken the ground there and been forgotten when the flood went down.

You come on deck in the morning; the sun is blazing

in the bright blue sky; the water is flat as a mill-pond—clear as a sheet of crystal. Sky-piercing mountains surround you, islands are scattered everywhere, but no main-

AMONG THE ISLANDS.

land is visible; yet much of what you see appears to be mainland, for the mountains are islands and the islands are mountains. Indeed it is almost impossible to tell where the mainland begins, and where the island-world ends.

The white mists of early morning are rolling over the deep—shrouding, partially concealing, partly disclosing, mingling with and ramifying everything, water and sky inclusive. On one side an island mountain, higher and grander than Ben Nevis, rears itself up so precipitously and looks down on the sea so frowningly, that it appears as if about to topple over on your head. On the other side a group of low skerries, bald and grey, just peep out above the level of the water, bespattered with and overshadowed by myriads of clamorous sea-gulls. You gaze out ahead, you glance over the stern, and behold similar objects and scenes endlessly repeated, and diversified.

The ascending sun scatters the mists, glitters on the sea, and converts the island world into gold. You almost shout with delight. You seize your sketch-book (if a painter), your note-book (if an author), and, with brush or pencil, note down your fervid impressions in glowing colours or in words that burn. Ten to one, however, you omit to note that a large proportion of the beauty in the midst of which you are revelling is transient, and owes its existence very much to *the weather*.

Another traveller passes through the same scenes under less favourable circumstances. The sky is grey, the mountains are grey, the water is grey or black, and a stiff breeze, which tips the wavelets with snow-white crests, causes him to feel disagreeably cold. The gulls are silent and melancholy; the sun is nowhere; perhaps a drizzle of rain makes the deck sloppy. The great island mountains are there, no doubt, but they are dismally, gloomily grand. The rocky islets are there too; but they look uncomfortable, and seem as if they would fain hide their heads in the troubled sea, in order to escape the gloom of the upper world.

The traveller groans and brushes away the raindrops that hang from the point of his lugubrious nose. If, in the eccentricity of despair, he should retire to the cabin, draw forth his note-book, and apply his stiffened fingers and chilled intellect to the task of composition, what does he write? "Detestable weather. Beauty of scenery absurdly overrated. Savage enough it is, truly; would that I were not in a like condition." Thus difference of opinion arises, and thus the non-travelling public is puzzled in its mind by the conflicting statements of men of unimpeachable veracity.

Through this island-world we sailed until the great mountain ranges of the interior became clearly visible, and as we gazed into the deep fiords we felt that that boldness and ruggedness so eminently characteristic of the old Norse vikings must have been fostered, if not created, by the scenery of their fatherland.

As we gazed and pondered, a huge old-fashioned ship came out suddenly from behind an island, as if to increase the archaic character of the scenery. There it was, undoubtedly (and there it may be seen every day), with the same high stempost as the galleys of old, only wanting a curve at the top and a dragon's head to make it complete,

ENTRANCE TO A FIORD.

and the same huge single mast with its one unwieldy square sail.

Presently a boat shot alongside and a sedate seaman stepped on board—a blue-eyed, fair-haired, sallow man with knee-breeches and long stockings, rough jacket, no vest, a red night-cap, and a glazed hat on the top of it. This was the pilot. He was a big, placid-looking man of about forty, with a slouching gait and a pair of immensely broad shoulders. We found that he had been away north for several weeks, piloting a vessel of some sort beyond the Arctic circle. He was now close to his home, but our signal had diverted him from his domestic leanings, and, like a thorough sea-monster, he prepared, at a moment's notice, for another voyage.

The obvious advantage that a yachter has over the voyager by steamboat is, that he can cast anchor when and where he pleases, and diverge from his course at will. Thus he discovers unsuspected points of interest and visits numberless spots of exquisite beauty, which, I verily believe, lie thickly hidden among these isles, as completely unknown to man (with the exception of a few obscure native fishermen in the neighbourhood) as are the vast solitudes of Central Africa. The yachter may sail for days, ay, for weeks, among these western islands, imbued with the romantic feelings of a Mungo Park, a Livingstone, or a Robinson Crusoe!

This is by no means a wild statement. When we consider the immense extent of the Norwegian coast, the innumerable friths of all sizes by which it is cut up, and the absolute impossibility of being certain as to whether the inlets which you pass in hundreds are fiords running into the main or mere channels between groups of islands, coupled with the fact that there is comparatively little traffic in the minor fiords except such as is carried on by native boats and barges, we can easily conceive that there are many dark friths along that coast which are as little

A FIORD SEEN FROM ABOVE.

known to travellers now, as they were in the days when Rolf Ganger issued from them with his vikings to conquer Normandy and originate those families from which have sprung the present aristocracy of England.

We ascended a fiord of this kind which we knew had not up to that time been visited, because there was a glacier at the head, which is mentioned by Professor

Forbes as being known only through native report—no traveller having seen it. This was the Skars fiord in lat. 67° N. The mere fact of this glacier being unknown, except by report, induced us to turn into the fiord with all the zest of explorers. A run of twelve miles brought us within sight of the object of our search, the first glance at which filled us with awe and admiration. But the longer we stayed and explored this magnificent "ice-river," the more were we amazed to find how inadequate were our first conceptions of its immense size.

Appearances here are to our eyes very deceptive, owing, doubtless, to our being unaccustomed to scenery of such grandeur and magnitude.

This glacier of the Skars fiord appeared to be only a quarter of a mile wide. On measuring the valley, which it entirely filled up, we found it to be nearly two miles in breadth. Its lower edge appeared to be a few feet thick, and about twenty yards or so from the sea, the shore of which was strewn with what appeared to be large stones.

On landing, we found that the space between the ice and the sea was upwards of half a mile in extent; the large stones turned out to be boulders, varying in size from that of a small boat to a large cottage; while the lower edge of the glacier itself was an irregular wall of ice about fifteen or twenty feet in height.

Standing at its base we looked up the valley over the fissured surface of the ice to that point where the white snow of its upper edge cut clear and sharp against the blue sky, and, after much consultation, we came to the

T

conclusion that it might be three or four miles from top to bottom. But, after wandering the whole day up the valley by the margin of the ice and carefully exploring it, we were forced to believe that it must be at least eight or ten miles in extent, and undoubtedly it was many hundreds of feet thick. When we reflect that this immense body of ice is only one of the many tongues which, descending the numerous valleys, carry off the overflow of the great *mer de glace* on the hill-tops of the interior, we can form some conception of the vast tract of Norwegian land that lies buried summer and winter under the ice.

There was a little blue spot in the glacier at a short distance from its lower edge which attracted our attention. On reaching it we found that it was a hole in the roof of the sub-glacial river.

The ice had recently fallen in, and I never beheld such intensely soft and beautiful blue colour as was displayed in the caverns thus exposed to view, varying from the faintest cerulean tinge to the deepest indigo. Immense masses of rock which had fallen from the cliffs lay scattered along the surface of the ice near the edge, and were being slowly transported towards the sea—so slowly, that probably months would pass before the smallest symptom of a change in position could be observed.

There were very few natives in this wild spot—so few that their presence did not in any appreciable degree affect the solitude and desolation of the scene. They

A COAST GLACIER.

expressed much surprise at seeing us, and said that travellers like ourselves had never been there before. Indeed, I have no doubt whatever that in many out-of-the-way places we were absolutely the first individuals of a class somewhat different from themselves that these poor Norse fishermen and small farmers of the coast had ever set eyes upon. Their looks of surprise in some cases, and of curiosity in all, showed this plainly enough.

In one chaotic glen or gorge where we landed we distributed a few presents among the people—such as knives, scissors, and thimbles—with which they were immensely delighted. Three of our party were ladies; and the curiosity exhibited by the Norse women in regard to our fair companions was very amusing. By the way, one of the said "fair" companions was a brunette, and her long jet black ringlets appeared to afford matter for unceasing wonder and admiration to the flaxen-haired maidens of Norway.

Of course I am now speaking of the untravelled districts. In the regular highways of the country, travellers of every class and nation are common enough. But Norway, in the interior as well as on the coast, has this advantage over other lands, that there are regions, plenty of them, where travellers have never been, and to reach which is a matter of so great difficulty that it is probable few will ever attempt to go. This fact is a matter of rejoicing in these days of railroads and steamboats!

NORWAY.

CHAPTER. II.

THE NATIVES AT HOME.

WHILE we were sailing up the Sogney fiord, which runs between stupendous mountains about a hundred miles into the interior of the country, we came to a gap in the mountains into which ran a branch of the fiord.

The spirit of discovery was strong upon my friend, the owner of the yacht, so he ordered our skipper to turn into it. We were soon running into as wild and gloomy a region as can well be conceived, with the mountains rising, apparently, straight up from the sea into the clouds, and tongues of the great Justedal glacier peeping over their summits. We turned into a large bay and cast anchor under the shadow of a hill more than 5,000 feet high.

Here we found the natives kind and hospitable; but,

indeed, this is the unvarying experience of travellers in Norway. They were not, in this fiord, like the poverty-stricken fishermen of the outer islands. They were a civilised, comfortable-looking, apparently well off, and altogether jovial race of people, some of whom took a deep interest in us, and overwhelmed us with kind attentions.

A NORWEGIAN CARRIAGE.

Their houses, which were built of wood, did not present much appearance of luxury, but there was no lack of all the solid comforts of life. No carpets covered the floors, and no paintings, except a few badly-coloured prints, graced the walls. But there were huge, quaint-looking stoves in every room, suggestive of a genial temperature; and there were scattered about numbers of immense meerschaum pipes and tobacco pouches, suggestive of fireside gossip—perchance legends and tales of the old sea-kings—in the long dark nights of winter.

I was strengthened here in my belief in the indissoluble connection between fat and good-humour; for all the people of this fiord seemed to me to be both good-humoured and fat. It was here, too, that I was for the first time strongly impressed with my own lamentable ignorance of the Norse language. Nevertheless, the old proverb—" Where there's a will there's a way "—held good, for the way in which I managed to hold converse with the natives of that region was astounding even to myself!

One bluff, hearty fellow of about fifty, with fair hair, a round, oily countenance, and bright blue eyes, took me off to see his wife and family. Up to this time our party had always kept together, and, being a lazy student, I had been wont to maintain a modest silence while some of my companions, more versed in the language, did all the talking. But now I found myself, for the first time, alone with a Norwegian!—fairly left to my own resources. Well, I began by stringing together all the Norse I knew (it was not much), and endeavouring to look as if I knew a great deal more. But I soon found that Murray's list of sentences did not avail me in a lengthened and desultory conversation.

My fat friend and I soon became very amicable and

communicative on this system. He told me innumerable stories of which I did not comprehend a sentence; but, nevertheless, I looked as if I did, smiled, nodded my head, and said " Ya, ya ;" to which he always replied, " Ya, ya," waving his arms and slapping his chest, and rolling his eyes, as he bustled along towards his dwelling.

The cottage was a curious little thing—a sort of huge toy, perched on a rock close to the water's edge. If it had slipped off that rock—a catastrophe which had at least the appearance of being possible—it would have plunged into forty or fifty fathoms of water, so steep were the hills and so deep the sea at that place. Here my friend found another subject to expatiate upon and dance round, in the shape of his own baby—a soft, smooth counterpart of himself—which lay sleeping like Cupid in its crib. The man was evidently extremely fond of this infant, not to say proud of it. He went quite into ecstasies about it; now gazing at it with looks of pensive admiration, anon starting and looking at me as if to say, " Did you ever in all your life behold such a beautiful cherub ?" The man's enthusiasm was really catching—I began to feel quite a paternal interest in the cherub myself.

" Oh ! " he cried in rapture, " det er smook bårn " (that a pretty baby).

" Ya, ya," said I, " megit smook " (very pretty), although I must confess that *smoked* bairn would have been equally appropriate, for it was as brown as a red-herring.

I spent an agreeable, though mentally confused, afternoon with this hospitable man and his two sisters,

PEASANTS AND MINISTER.

who were placid, fat, amiable, and fair. They gave me the impression of having never been in a condition of haste or perturbation from their birthdays up to that time. We sat in a sort of small garden, round a green painted table, drinking excellent coffee, of which beverage the Norwegians seem to be uncommonly fond.

The costume of these good people was of an uncommonly sombre hue; indeed, this is the case throughout Norway generally. But when a Norse girl marries, she comes out for once in brilliant plumage. She decks herself out in the gaudiest of habiliments, with a profusion of gold and silver ornaments. The most conspicuous part of her costume is a crown of pure silver, gilt, and a scarlet-cloth breast-piece, which is thickly studded with silver-gilt brooches and beads of various hues, besides little round mirrors! This breast-piece and the crown usually belong, not to the bride, but to the district! They are a species of public property hired out by each bride on her wedding-day for the sum of about five shillings. This costume is gorgeous, and remarkably becoming, especially when worn by a fair-haired, blue-eyed, and pretty Norse girl.

Some time after the little touch of domestic life above narrated, we had a specimen of the manner in which the peasants of these remote glens indulge in a little public recreation. We chanced to be up at the head of the Nord fiord on the eve of St. John's day, not the day of the Evangelist, but of the Baptist. This is a great day in Norway; and poor indeed must be the hamlet where, on the eve of that day, there is not an attempt made to kindle a mighty blaze and make merry. On St. John's Eve, bonfires leap and roar over the length and breadth of the land.

The manner in which the people rejoiced upon this occasion was curious and amusing. But here I must turn aside for one moment to guard myself from misconstruction. It needs little reasoning to prove that where the mountains rise something like walls into the clouds, and are covered with everlasting ice, the inhabitants of the valleys may have exceedingly little intercourse with each other. The doings on this occasion may or may not have been peculiar, in some points, to this particular valley at the head of the Nord fiord. I simply describe what I saw.

It was midnight when we went to a field at the base of a mountain to witness the rejoicings of the people. But the midnight hour wore not the sombre aspect of night in our more southerly climes. The sun had indeed set, but the blaze of his refulgent beams still shot up into the zenith, and sent a flood of light over the whole sky. In fact, it was almost broad daylight, and the only change that took place that night was the gradual increasing of the light as the sun rose again, at a preposterously early hour, to recommence his long-continued journey through the summer sky.

Assembled on the greensward of the field, and surrounded by mountains whose summits were snow-capped and whose precipitous sides were seamed with hundreds of cataracts that gushed from frozen caves, were upwards of a thousand men and women. There seemed to me to be comparatively few children.

AT THE HEAD OF THE NORD FIORD.

To give a pretty fair notion of the aspect of this concourse, it is necessary to give an account of only two individual units thereof. One man wore a dark brown pair of coarse homespun trousers, a jacket and vest of the same material, and a bright scarlet cap, such as fishermen are wont to wear. One woman wore a dark coarse gown and a pure white kerchief on her head tied under her chin. There were some slight modifications, no doubt, but the multiplication of those two by a thousand gives very nearly the desired result. The men resembled a crop of enormous poppies, and the women a crop of equally gigantic lilies.

Yet, although the brilliancy of the red and white was intense, the deep sombreness of the undergrowth was overpowering. There was a dark rifle-corps-like effect about them at a distance, which—albeit suggestive of pleasing military memories in these volunteering days— was in itself emphatically dismal.

Having come there to enjoy themselves, these good people set about the manufacture of enjoyment with that grave, quiet, yet eminently cheerful demeanour, which is a characteristic feature of most of the country people of Norway whom I have seen. They had delayed commencing operations until our arrival. Several of the older men came forward and shook hands with us very heartily, after which they placed three old boats together and covered them outside and in with tar, so that when the torch was applied there was such a sudden blaze of light as dimmed the lustre of the midnight sun himself for a time.

Strange to say, no enthusiasm seemed to kindle in the

breasts of the peasants. A careless observer would have deemed them apathetic, but this would have been a mistaken opinion. They evidently looked on the mighty blaze with *calm* felicity. Their enjoyment was clearly a matter of fact; it may have been deep, it certainly was not turbulent.

Soon we heard a sound resembling the yells of a pig. This was a violin. It was accompanied by a noise resembling the beating of a flour-mill, which, we found, proceeded from the heel of the musician, who had placed a wooden board under his left foot for the purpose of beating time with effect. He thus, as it were, played the fiddle and beat the drum at the same time.

Round this musician the young men and maidens formed a ring and began to dance. There was little talking, and that little was in an undertone. They went to work with the utmost gravity and decorum. Scarcely a laugh was heard—nothing approaching to a shout during the whole night—nevertheless, they enjoyed themselves thoroughly; I have no doubt whatever of that.

The nature of their dances was somewhat incomprehensible. It seemed as if the chief object of the young men was to exhibit their agility by every species of impromptu bound and fling of which the human frame is capable, including the rather desperate feat of dashing themselves flat upon the ground. The principal care of the girls seemed to be to keep out of the way of the men and avoid being killed by a frantic kick or felled by a random blow. But the desperate features in each dance did not appear at first

Every man began by seizing his partner's hand, and dragging her round the circle, ever and anon twirling her round violently with one arm, and catching her

round the waist with the other, in order—as it appeared to me—to save her from an untimely end. To this treatment the fair damsels submitted with pleased though bashful looks.

But soon the men flung them off, and went at it entirely on their own account; yet they kept up a sort of revolving course round their partners, like satellites encircling their separate suns. Presently the satellites assumed some of the characteristics of the comet. They rushed about the circle in wild erratic courses; they leaped into the air, and, while in that position, slapped the soles of their feet with both hands. Should any one deem this an easy feat, let him try it.

Then they became a little more sane, and a waltz, or something like it, was got up. It was really pretty, and some of the movements were graceful; but the wild spirit of the glens re-entered the men rather suddenly. The females were expelled from the ring altogether, and the youths braced themselves for a little really heavy work; they flung and hurled themselves about like maniacs, stood on their heads and walked on their hands—in short, became a company of acrobats, yet always kept up a sympathetic feeling for time with the music. But not a man, woman, or child there gave vent to his or her feelings in laughter!

They smiled; they commented in a soft tone; they looked happy—nay, I am convinced they *were* happy—but they did not laugh. Once only did they give vent to noisy mirth, and that was when an aspiring youth (after having made the nearest possible approach to suicide) walked round the circle on his hands and shook his feet in the air. We left them, after a time, in the full swing of a prosperous manufacture of enjoyment, and walked home, about two o'clock in the morning, by brilliant daylight.

NORWAY.

CHAPTER III.

THE NATIVES ABROAD.

WHILST travelling from place to place by steamer one enjoys many opportunities of studying the character and habits of the people.

I chanced, once, to be the only Briton on board the steamer that plied between the Nord fiord and Bergen, and I was particularly struck, on that occasion, with the *silence* that seemed to be cultivated by the people as if it were a virtue. I do not mean to say that the passengers and crew were taciturn—far from it; they bustled about actively, and were quite sociable and talkative; but all their talk was in an undertone—no voice was ever raised to a loud pitch. Even the captain, when he gave orders, did so in a quiet voice, usually walking up to the men and telling them gently to do so and so. When I called to mind the bellowing of our own nautical men, this seemed to me a remarkably modest way of getting on, and very different from what one might have expected from the descendants of the rough vikings of old.

The prevailing quiescence, however, reached its culminating point at the dinner table, for there the silence was *total*, although a good deal of gesticulative ceremony and vigorous muscular action prevailed. When we had all assembled in the cabin at the whispered request of the steward, and had stood for a few minutes looking benign and expectant, *but not talking*, the captain entered, bowed to the company, was bowed to by the company, motioned us to our seats, whispered "*ver so goot*," and sat down.

This phrase *ver so goot* (I spell it as pronounced) merits explanation in passing. It is an expression that seems to me capable of extension and distension, and is frequently on the lip of a Norwegian. It is a convenient, flexible, jovial expression, which is easily said, easily remembered, and means much. I cannot think of a better way of conveying an idea of its signification than by saying that it is a compound of the phrases, "be so good"—"by your leave"—"if you please"—"go it, my hearties"—and "that's your sort." The first of these, *be so good*, is the literal translation, the remainder are the superinduced sentiments resulting from the tone and manner in which the words are uttered. You may rely upon it that when a Norwegian offers you anything and says "*rer so goot*," he means you well, and hopes you will make yourself comfortable.

But, to return to our dinner party. There was no carving at this meal—a circumstance worthy of consideration and imitation. The dishes were handed round by waiters. First of all we had sweet rice soup with wine and raisins in it, the eating of which seemed to me like the spoiling of one's dinner with a bad pudding. This finished, the plates were removed.

The silence had by this time begun to impress me. "Now," thought I, "surely some one will converse with his neighbour during this interval." No; not a lip moved! I glanced at my right and left hand men. I thought for a moment of venturing out upon the unknown deep of a foreign tongue, and cleared my throat; but every eye was on me in an instant, and the sound of my own voice, even in that familiar process, was so appalling that I subsided. I looked at the pretty girl opposite me. I felt certain that the young fellow next her was on the point of addressing her, but I was mistaken. Either he had forgotten what he meant to say, or his thoughts were too big for utterance. I am still under the impression that this youth would have broken the ice had not the next course come on and claimed his undivided attention.

The second course began with a dish like bread pudding, minus currants and raisins—suggesting the idea that these ameliorative elements had been put into the soup by mistake. It looked as if it were a sweet dish, but it turned out to be salt; and pure melted butter, without any admixture of flour and water, was handed round as sauce. After this came veal and beef cutlets, which we ate mixed with cranberry jam, pickles, and potatoes. Then came the concluding course—cold sponge cake, with almonds and raisins scattered over it. By this arrangement we were enabled, after eating the cake as pudding, to slide naturally and pleasantly into dessert without a change of plates.

There was a general tendency in the company to bend their heads over, and rather close to, their plates while eating, as if for the purpose of communing privately with the viands, and a particular tendency on the part of the man next me to spread his arms and thrust one of his elbows into my side, in regard to which I exercised much forbearance. The only beverages used, besides cold water, were table beer and St. Julien, the latter a thin acid wine much used in Norway; but there was no drinking after dinner. It seemed to be the etiquette to rise from table simultaneously. We did so on this occasion, and then a general process of bowing ensued.

In regard to this latter proceeding I have never been able to arrive at a clear understanding as to what was actually done or intended to be done, but my impression is, that each bowed to the other, and all bowed to the captain; then the captain bowed to each individually, and to all collectively; after which a comprehensive bow was made by everybody to all the rest all round, and then we went on deck. In fact, it seemed as if the effect of dinner had been to fill each man with such overflowing benignity and goodwill that he would have smiled and bowed to a bedpost had it come in his way, and I am certain that the obliging waiters came in for a large share of these civilities, and repaid the company in kind.

As each guest passed out, he or she said to the captain, "*tak for mad.*" This is a "manner and custom," throughout all Norway, and means *thanks for meat*. The expression is usually accompanied with a shake of the host's hand, but that part of the ceremony was not performed upon this occasion, probably because the captain was not a *bona fide* host, seeing that we had paid for our dinner. With the exception of these three words at the end, and "*ver so goot*" at the beginning, not a single syllable was uttered by any one during the whole course of that meal.

When the deck was gained the gentlemen immediately took to smoking. As a matter of course, Norwegians smoke, and they entertain enlarged ideas on that subject, if one may judge from the immense size of their meerschaums, and the large fat tobacco-pouch that is worn by every man, strapped across his shoulders.

There was a youth in this steamer— a beardless youth —whose first thought in the morning, and whose last glimmer of an idea at night, was his pipe, the bowl of which was as large as his own fist.

I remember watching him with deep interest. He was

long, cadaverous, and lanky—in these respects unlike his countrymen. He slept on the sofa just opposite the spot whereon I lay, so that, unless I turned my face to the side of the vessel or shut my eyes, he was an unavoidable subject of contemplation. On awaking he stretched himself, which act had an alarming appearance in one so long by nature, and so attenuated. Then he filled his pipe with an air of deep abstraction and profound melancholy—the result, I suppose, of his being unrefreshed by his recent slumbers.

Of course, no one of sense would think of attributing this to excessive smoking!

The pipe filled, he arose; on rising, he lit it; while dressing, he smoked it; and till breakfast it burned fiercely like a blast-furnace. During the morning meal it went out, but before the big bowl had time to cool it was rekindled. He smoked till dinner-time; dined, and smoked till tea-time; tea'd, and smoked till bed-time. Then he lay down for the night, and still continued to smoke until I or he, I forget which, fell asleep. He awoke before I did next morning, so that when I opened my eyes the first object they rested on was the bowl of that youth's meerschaum enveloped in clouds of smoke!

I am tempted to moralise, but I refrain. Mankind is smitten with the disease, and I am afraid that it is incurable.

NORWAY.

CHAPTER IV.

DAY AND NIGHT.

THE farther north you go in voyaging along the coast during the months of June and July the brighter and longer becomes the daylight, until at last you arrive at the regions of perpetual day.

The charm of this state of things is beyond the comprehension of those who have not experienced it. Apart altogether from the gladdening influence of sunshine, there is something delightfully reckless in the feeling that there is no necessity whatever for taking note of the flight of time—no fear lest we should, while wandering together, or perchance alone, among the mountains, be overtaken by night. During several weeks we lived in the blaze of a long nightless day.

While we were in this bright region most of us laid

aside our watches as useless, leaving it, if I remember rightly, to the skipper of our yacht to tell us when Sunday came round, for we always, when practicable, spent that day at anchor, and had service on board.

I do not use hyperbolical language when speaking of this perpetual daylight. During several weeks, after we had crossed the Arctic circle, the sun descended little more than its own diameter below the horizon each night, so that it had scarcely set when it rose again, and the diminution of the light was quite insignificant; it did not approach in the slightest degree to twilight. If I had suddenly awakened during any of the twenty-four hours in the cabin of the yacht, or in any place from which it was impossible to observe the position of the sun, I could not have told whether it was night or day!

Having said that, it is almost superfluous to add that we could, even in the cabin, read the smallest print at midnight as easily as at noonday. Moreover, a clear midnight was absolutely brighter than a cloudy forenoon. Nevertheless, there was a distinct difference between night and day—a difference with which light had nothing to do.

I am inclined to think that the incalculable myriads of minute and invisible creatures with which God has filled the solitudes of this world, even more largely than its inhabited parts, exercise a much more powerful influence on our senses than we suppose.

During the day-time these teeming millions, bustling about in the activities of their tiny spheres, create an actual, though unrecognisable noise. I do not refer to gnats and flies so much as to those atomic insects whose little persons are never seen, and whose individual voices are never heard, but whose collective hum is a fact that is best proved by the silence that follows its cessation.

In the evening these all retire to rest, and night is marked by a deep impressive stillness, which we are apt erroneously to suppose is altogether the result of that noisy giant man having betaken himself to his lair. Yet this difference between night and day was only noticeable when we were alone, or very quiet; the preponderating noises resulting from conversation or walking were more than sufficient to dispel the sweet influence.

We were often very far wrong in our ideas of time. Once or twice, on landing and going into a hamlet on the coast, we have been much surprised to find the deepest silence reigning everywhere, and, on peeping in at a window, to observe that the inhabitants were all in bed, while the sun was blazing high in the heavens.

Sometimes, too, on returning from a shooting or fishing expedition, I have seen a bush or a tree full of small birds, each standing on one leg, with its head thrust under its wing and its round little body puffed up to nearly twice its usual size, and have thus been reminded that the hours for rest had returned. Of course a little observation and reflection would at any time have cleared up our minds as to whether day or night was on the wing—

nevertheless, I state the simple truth when I say that we were often much perplexed, and sometimes ludicrously deceived, by the conversion of night into day.

On one occasion we lay becalmed in a fiord somewhere beyond the Arctic circle. It was fine weather, but the

AN HOUR AFTER MIDNIGHT.

sky was not so bright as usual, being obscured by clouds. A fisherman's boat happening to pass, we resolved to take advantage of it and escape the monotony of a calm by having a row up the fiord. The fisherman said there was a good salmon river and plenty of ptarmigan at a place little more than a Norse mile off—equal to about seven English miles—so we took rods and guns with us. It was evening when we set forth, but I did not know the exact hour.

The scenery through which we passed at this particular place was on a smaller scale than is usual in Norway, and we enjoyed our row more than usual in consequence; scenery on a small scale is more enjoyable than scenery on a large scale; the reason of this seems to be that, when in the midst of scenery on a small scale, the traveller is constantly and rapidly presented with new views, as well as with beautiful and varied combinations of the same views, while in that on a large scale the eye becomes indifferent to the almost changeless grandeur of prospects which are so vast that they are necessarily presented to the view for hours at a time.

On our way we met with a Finn. He stood on a rock, gazing at us with much interest. I know not in what circle of Finnish society this individual moved, but his class and tribe had certainly no reason to be proud of his personal appearance. He was diminutive, dishevelled, and dirty. His dress was a leathern tunic, belted round the waist; his leggings were of the same material. But the most conspicuous portion of his costume was a tall, conical worsted night-cap, which we neatly, but accidentally, knocked off his head with a piece of tobacco. He looked angry at first, but on becoming aware of the nature and quality of our missile, his weather-beaten visage beamed with forgiving smiles.

Next we came **upon** an eagle, which alighted on a tree and allowed us to come within long range—at least **our** sanguine temperaments induced **us to** hope that it was long range—before taking **flight. Of course it** took no notice whatever of the **three shots we fired at it.** Soon after **that we reached the mouth of the river.**

Here **we found a small hamlet of** exceedingly poor people, who received **us hospitably, but** with such evident astonishment, that **we** concluded they had never seen civilised visitors before. Their fiord was off the track of steamers, and far distant from any **town. They** themselves were little if at all better than **North** American Indians.

They gathered round us with open **eyes** and mouths, and the women handled our clothes with evident wonder. We presented them with several **pairs of** scissors, whereupon they shook **hands** with us **all round** and said "*tak*" —thanks—very **heartily.** In **this custom** of shaking **hands** when a gift is presented, **I** usually found that **the** receiver shook hands not only **with** the donor, but, **in** the exuberance of his gratitude, **with** the whole party.

The looks **of the people** betokened either that scissors were entirely **new implements to them,** or that those we presented were **of** unusually good **quality.** They went about snipping everything in the **most** reckless manner. **One woman caught** hold of **the ends of** her daughter's **neckerchief and snipped them** both off; whereupon her husband plucked them out of her hand, and snipped off the ends of his beard.

Here, the huts being dirty, we picnicked on the greensward. We had brought tea and biscuit with us, and the natives supplied us with some thick sour milk with half an inch of sour cream on it—a dish which is common all over Norway, and is much relished by the people as well as by many of their visitors.

This disposed of, we set out—some to fish, and others to shoot. I went off alone with my gun. Ptarmigan, in summer plumage, which is brown, with pure white feathers intermixed, were numerous, but wild. They were just tame enough to lead me on in an excited and hopeful state of mind for several hours, regardless of the flight of time.

At last I became tired, and having bagged four or five birds I returned to the boat, where I found my comrades. One of them chanced to have a watch, and from him I learned that it was just two o'clock in the morning! so that I had actually been shooting all night by daylight; and the sun had set and risen again without my being aware of the fact. We did not get back to the yacht till eight o'clock A.M., when we found the crew just sitting down to a breakfast of oatmeal porridge. Some of us having refreshed ourselves with a dip in the sea, took a plate of this. Then we went to bed, and rose again at six o'clock that evening to breakfast.

During one of my solitary rambles with the gun, I had the good fortune to shoot a magnificent eagle. I say good fortune advisedly, because the eagle is so wary that few sportsmen succeed in killing one, and those who do have more cause to be thankful for their luck than proud of their prowess. It happened thus: About two o'clock one beautful morning in July I lay wide awake in my berth, looking up through the skylight at the bright blue heavens; the yacht being becalmed somewhere between latitudes 64° and 65°, and the sun having commenced to ascend the vault from which it had disappeared for only half an hour.

On that night—if I may be permitted the inappropriate expression—I could not sleep. I counted the hours as they passed slowly by; practised without success the various little devices that are erroneously supposed to bring slumber to the sleepless; grew desperate, and finally jumped up at four a.m., resolving to row myself to the nearest island and shoot. There were usually eider ducks in the little creeks, and ptarmigan among the scrub. Should these fail me I could vent my spleen on the gulls.

Arming myself with a double-barrel, I quaffed a tumbler of water and sallied forth, ignorant of the fact that it contained a large dose of morphia, which had been prescribed for an ailing but refractory member of our party the previous evening. No one was stirring. It was a dead calm.

Landing on a lovely island, of perhaps five or six miles in extent, which rose in the form of a rugged mountain to a height of about 4,000 feet, I rambled for some time among low bushes and wild flowers, but found no game. The gulls, as if aware of my intentions, had forsaken the low rocks, and were flying high up among the precipices and serried ridges and peaks of the mountain. Resolved not to be discomfited I began to ascend, and as I mounted upward the splendour of the island scenery became more apparent. The virtuous feelings consequent upon early rising induced a happy frame of mind, which was increased by the exhilarating influence of the mountain air.

It was a wild lonesome place, full of deep dark gorges and rugged steeps, to clamber up which, if not a work of danger, was at least one of difficulty. While I stood on a rocky ledge, gazing upwards at the sinuosities of the ravine above me, I observed a strange apparition near the edge of a rock about forty yards off. It was a face, a red, hairy, triangular visage, with a pair of piercing black eyes, that gazed down upon me in unmitigated amazement. The gun flew to my shoulder; I looked steadily for a moment; the eyes winked; *bang!* went the gun, and when the smoke cleared away the eyes and head were gone. Clambering hastily up the cliff, I found a red fox lying dead behind a rock.

Bagging Reynard, I ascended the giddy heights where the gulls were circling. Here the clouds enshrouded me occasionally as they sailed past, making the gulls loom gigantic. Suddenly an enormous bird swooped past me, looking so large in the white mist that I felt assured it must be an eagle. I squatted behind a rock at once, and as the mists cleared away a few minutes later I saw him clearly enough sailing high up in the sky. I glanced down at the yacht that lay like a speck on the water far below, and up at the noble bird that went soaring higher and higher every moment, and I felt a species of awe

THE EAGLE.

creep over me when I thought of the tremendous gulf of space that lay between that eagle and the world below.

He was evidently bent on making closer acquaintance with some of the gulls, so I sat down behind a rock to watch him. But knowing the shyness and sharp-sightedness of the bird I soon gave up all hope of getting a shot. Presently he made a rapid circling flight downwards, and, after hovering a few minutes, alighted on a cliff several hundred yards distant from my place of concealment. Hope at once revived; I rose, and began, with the utmost caution, to creep towards him. The rugged nature of the ground favoured my approach, else I should never have succeeded in evading the glance of his bold and watchful eye.

When I had approached to within about eighty or ninety yards, I came to an open space, across which it was impossible to pass without being seen. This was beyond conception vexing. To lose him when almost within my grasp was too bad! I thought of trying a long shot, but feeling certain that it would be useless, I prepared, as a last resource, to make a sudden rush towards him and get as near as possible before he should rise.

The plan was successful. Cocking both barrels I darted out of my place of concealment with the wild haste of a maniac, and, before the astonished eagle could launch himself off the cliff, I had lessened the distance between us by at least thirty yards. Then I took rapid aim, and fired both barrels almost simultaneously.

I might as well, apparently, have discharged a pop-gun at him. Not a quiver of wing or tail took place. He did not even accelerate his majestic flight, as the shots reverberated from cliff to cliff, and I watched him sail slowly round a crag and disappear. Re-loading, I sauntered in moody desperation in the direction of his flight, and soon gained the point round which he had vanished, when, behold! he lay on the ground with his broad wings expanded to their full extent and his head erect. I ran towards him, but he did not move, and I soon saw that he was mortally wounded. On coming close up I was compelled to halt and gaze at him in admiration. He raised his head and looked at me with a glance of lofty disdain which I shall never forget.

The conformation of the eagle's eye is such that its habitual expression, as every one knows, resembles that of deep indignation. This bird had that look in perfection. His hooked beak was above four inches long, and it struck me that if he were disposed to make a last gallant struggle for life when I grasped him, such a beak, with its corresponding talons, would give me some ugly wounds before I could master him. I therefore laid my gun gently across his back and held him down therewith while I caught him by the neck. But his fighting days were over. His head drooped forward and his bold eye closed in death a few seconds later.

Afterwards I found that the whole charge of both barrels had lodged in his body and thighs, yet, on receiving this, he did not wince a hair's breadth, or in any other way indicate that he had been touched. He measured exactly six feet six inches across the expanded wings.

Alas! his stuffed skin, which I have preserved as a

Norwegian trophy, gives but a feeble idea of what the bird was when, in all the fire of strength, courage, and freedom, he soared above the mountain peaks of Norway.

PRINTED BY VIRTUE AND CO., LIMITED, CITY ROAD, LONDON.

www.ingramcontent.com/pod-product-compliance
Lightning Source LLC
Chambersburg PA
CBHW030753230426
43667CB00007B/956